Love Does No Harm

LOVE DOES NO HARM

Sexual Ethics for the Rest of Us

Marie M. Fortune

Foreword by M. Joycelyn Elders, M.D.

Preface by James B. Nelson

continuum

NEW YORK • LONDON

2003

The Continuum International Publishing Group Inc
15 East 26th Street, New York, NY 10010

Printed in the United States of America

Library of Congress Cataloging-in-Publication Data

Fortune, Marie M.
    Love does no harm : sexual ethics for the rest of us / Marie M. Fortune ; foreword by M. Joycelyn Elders, M.D.; preface by James B. Nelson.
         p.   cm.
    Includes bibliographical references (p.   ) and index.
    ISBN 0-8264-1128-2 (paperback : acid-free paper)
    1. Sexual ethics. 2. Sexual ethics for women.
  3. Women—Sexual behavior. 4. Men—Sexual behavior.
  5. Interpersonal relations. 6. Feminist theory. I. Title.
HQ32.F69   1995   95-3731
306.7—dc20   CIP

The author and publisher gratefully acknowledge permission to reprint the following material in this book:

Excerpts from Nicola Gavey. "Technologies and Effects of Heterosexual Coercion," in Heterosexuality: A Feminism and Psychology Reader, Wilkinson and Ketzinger, eds., copyright 1993 by Sage Publications, Inc. Reprinted by permission of Sage Publications, Inc.

Excerpts from June Larkin and Katherine Popaleni, "Heterosexual Courtship, Violence, and Sexual Harassment: The Private and Public Control of Young Women," in Feminism and Psychology, Vol. 4, No. 2 (May, 1994) by Sage Publications, Ltd. Reprinted by permission of Sage Publications, Ltd.

Excerpts from Refusing to be a Man, by John Stoltenberg, reprinted by permission of John Stoltenberg, copyright John Stoltenberg, 1990.

Excerpts from Kathleen Fleming, "Checkpoint: A Lovers' Game," in Lesbian Bedtime Stories 2, Terry Woodrow, ed., 1990, Tough Dove Books. Reprinted by permission.

for
Vanessa, Rachel, Elena, Nicole, Sasha,
Douglas, Benjamin, Hannah, Sophia, and Jeremy
in the hope that they will find relationships rooted
in justice and love, equality and respect.

✼

Two are better than one, because they have a good reward for their toil. For if they fall, one will lift up the other; but woe to one who is alone and falls and does not have another to help. Again, if two lie together, they keep warm; but how can one keep warm alone?

—Ecclesiastes 4:9–11 NRSV

∞

I am eleven years old and entirely too young to hear about it. Can you imagine my mother not knowing what Kotex are for and dusting the house with them? Well, her mother can just tell her what they are for, I'm not getting into the facts of life. I haven't heard one fact of life that I liked yet.

—Daisy Fay in *Daisy Fay and the Miracle Man* by Fannie Flagg

Contents

Foreword

⚡ It is encouraging that Marie M. Fortune brings you this new work, *Loves Does No Harm: Sexual Ethics for the Rest of Us*.

While intimate relationships have always been problematic, it seems in recent years we are witnessing a great deal of breakdown in our society. We are seeing a growing trend toward more violence, teen pregnancy, sexually transmitted diseases, and dependency on drugs and alcohol. In so many instances, relationships just do not seem to be what they should. Too many people have been left in a state of pain, shame, denial, helplessness, and hopelessness (including our children). Marie Fortune suggests this situation may stem in part from a basic lack of ethics in too many of our decisions and choices—choices which affect not only the individual, but also those whose lives are touched by the individual. The suggestion is thought provoking.

The reader may not be in total agreement with everything stated or suggested in the work—as I am not. But we must realize that now, more than ever, it is crucial to the overall health and well-being of all people that we be open to expanding our understanding and educating ourselves so we can eventually reach the goal of finding healthy solutions to our societal and physical ills. This book will serve in some way to help meet this vast need for more education and reflection on our behavior, individually and collectively.

M. JOYCELYN ELDERS, M.D.
JANUARY 1995

Preface

∞ It is a privilege to introduce Marie M. Fortune's book because I find its approach to sexual ethics one of great strength and enormous usefulness.

This is a realistic book. It recognizes the ambiguities of the relationships in which we actually live (always refreshing in books on ethics, I might add!). The author does not simplify our sexual complexities, nor does she minimize the hard and courageous work required by our decisions. But she trusts us enough to provide guidelines, not rigid rules. Then she lavishly illustrates the ways in which real people struggle with those guidelines, and readers will surely find themselves in these pages. In short, this is a book that nourishes our capacity for ethical discernment—the ability to choose actions that embody our values, with eyes wide open to the consequences of our choices.

The book is inclusive. Fortune is speaking to all people regardless of their orientations or relational configurations. It is also inclusive because, while based on her own Christian feminist assumptions, this ethical approach is accessible to anyone concerned about justice, integrity, and fulfillment in their intimate lives. Furthermore, these sexual matters, she rightly notes, are not limited to people of white, North American privilege. While the contexts of experience may vary greatly, these persisting human issues cut across all lines of race, class, and ethnicity.

The book is theologically realistic. While its central norm is love, there is no sentimentality here. That is imperative, for distorted perceptions of love have been used as the justification for much abuse. Marie Fortune knows that well, for as a pioneering leader in the struggle against sexual violence, she hears such stories daily. Thus, she has an unblinking realism about our human sin. She is realistic about the ways in which the patriarchal patterns of dominance and submission still pervade our culture, infusing the possibility of emotional and physical violence into every relationship, even for gay and lesbian couples. And her realism keeps the issues of power, consent, and the resources for action ever before us.

For all its realism, this is a profoundly hopeful book. Though, as Fortune admits, "doing least harm" can be understood as a minimalist or even negative ethic, in her understanding it is not so. She chooses this principle not only because it honestly recognizes the harm so pervasive in intimate relationships, but also because she knows we are capable of following this standard. That is hopeful.

The author believes that we are capable of embracing the important guidelines that bring content to this principle: relative equality in power, authentic consent, stewardship and safety, the sharing of pleasure, and faithfulness. Indeed, the perceptive way she unpacks each of these relational norms provides not only guidance for our perplexities but also enriching material for the renewal of our commitments.

It is a hopeful book because of the incarnational theology that underlies it. While it is not the author's chosen task to theologize about sexuality, it is transparently clear she believes that God is truly experienced in the midst of those everyday relationships that are authentically loving. She knows that as human beings we are so radically relational that our loves of God, self, and neighbor (the partner) are finally inseparable. Self-love is necessary grounding for love of the partner, and when we truly love another human being we are at the same time loving God.

I find this book deeply hopeful because of the assumptions about our human nature that I find on every page. Through her significant ministry, Marie Fortune knows better than most how capable we are of doing great harm in our sexual relationships. Even more fundamentally, she knows that our very nature makes us desire intimacy. We are created hungry for connection. We are fated with the will to communion. Our fundamental human craving is to belong, and our root anxiety is that of not belonging. God is love, and we are destined to be lovers.

Correspondingly, our sin is estrangement from love, life in which fulfilling connection is broken, life in which our choices express our lives in distorted ways. And our distorted loves become systemic, embedded in our institutions. The personal is public. However, even when our loves are destructively distorted, they strangely reveal our intended destiny. Our most warped and harmful loves are still desperate attempts to find connection. I believe that such an understanding of human nature paradoxically gives solid hope for our human transformation.

Finally, this book is hopeful because it is erotic. Fortune knows well how important *eros* is—our hunger for pleasurable and fulfilling connections. If patriarchy tenaciously persists because patterns of dominance and submission have been eroticized, our hope lies in eroticizing patterns of sexual justice and mutuality. Indeed, it is the design of God that truly fulfilling pleasure comes only in such relationships. So, the author often graces her pages with delightful poetic sensuousness, an important contribution to that socially transformative end.

W. H. Auden often reminded us that it is the pleasure haters who become unjust. But the ancient Hebrew love poet (whom the author happily quotes) reminds us that, even in the midst of an often unjust and violent world, the Cosmic Lover might still meet us in the flesh of our days. We are given a vision that the winter shall be past, the flowers shall appear on the earth, the time of singing shall come, and the voice of the turtle dove shall be heard in the land. Marie Fortune's book is an important contribution toward that vision.

JAMES B. NELSON

Acknowledgments

∽ BECAUSE A PROJECT LIKE THIS is invariably collaborative, I want to acknowledge the valuable feedback and support which I received from Frances Wood, Kathleen Carlin, Emilie Townes, Debra Jarvis, Elizabeth Carlin, Rebecca Voekel-Haugen, Sandra Barone, Joe Leonard, Nicole Barone, Gary Wilson, Alison Webster, Julie Spitzer, Beth Basham, Sandy Butler, Dale Sewall, Jim Poling, Larry Graham, Eldon Olson, Gus Kaufman, and Anne Ganley. Their thoughtful questions and comments moved me forward. I want to thank the Board and staff of the Center for the Prevention of Sexual and Domestic Violence for their support and for sabbatical time for focused work. I also want to thank Savannah and Santeetlah for their steadfast presence.

I am most grateful to my friend and colleague Mary Hunt for her careful and critical suggestions and especially to Carol Adams whose tireless empathy and critical feedback were invaluable. They both encourage and support my clarity of thought and expression.

Finally much gratitude to my editor, Cynthia Eller, who understood and appreciated this project from the beginning and whose skill as a midwife brought it to fruition.

Introduction

∽ IN THE SPRING OF 1992, as I was perusing the women's magazine section of a local convenience store, interested in discovering
what topics were currently being covered for women, I picked up
a copy of *Glamour*. I checked the table of contents and discovered
a regular column called "Sexual Ethics." Fascinated that such an
approach existed in this particular magazine, I immediately turned
to the article and found an extensive discussion for women on the
parallels between choosing a man and shopping. "Sometimes we
shop for men the way we shop for clothing, accessories or even
household appliances—with checklists prepared and pencils at
the ready. We are often concerned about how well a particular
man will go with whatever we already have in our psychological
and social closets."[1] Though I have no problem about women
carefully considering with whom they wish to enter into relationships, to suggest that this discussion had anything to do with
ethics was not only grossly superficial, but also insulting to both
women and men.

The mixture of feelings which welled up in me is hard to
describe: astonishment and disbelief headed the list. But outrage
was close behind. Is this the sum of what we have to offer young
women who are faced with increasingly complex decision making
about sexuality and relationships? This was the last straw which
convinced me that someone should be writing about ethics for
real people, about making decisions and choices which affect not
only the individual but those whose lives are touched by that
individual. That someone might as well be me.

I come to this task as a Christian feminist pastor and educator whose ministry has focused on naming the sin of sexual violence and seeking healing and justice in its aftermath. In this role I have listened to countless stories from women and men about their experiences as victims of abuse. I have heard their pain and confusion, anger and disillusionment. Most of them had been victimized by someone close to them. Many of them wonder, if an intimate relationship is possible without abuse. How can they ever trust anyone enough to be intimate with them? These are questions which confront us all. In this book, I would like to engage in a constructive effort to suggest ways that we, as adult decision makers, can exercise our best judgment and bring our best selves to an intimate relationship.

As a society, we have all but abandoned the responsibility to equip people with the skills to make serious ethical choices. The right wing continues to promote "family values" as the answer to every problem. This is only a thinly veiled code phrase suggesting that whatever happens in heterosexual marriage is good. This underlying presumption only works if one is never confronted with real problems and choices. The so-called Christian right also presumes that the only real Christians are those who are anti-abortion, anti-gay, and anti-feminism. This is not true, but they succeed in their propaganda campaign because they are filling a vacuum left when many of our religious and community leaders, lacking courage and imagination, have remained virtually speechless in the face of critical ethical questions about sexuality and relationships.

This book also is about "family values"—the values we bring to and derive from our intimate relationships: values like respect, honesty, love, loyalty, safety, acceptance, and support. It is about how we can make sometimes difficult choices which are consistent with these values. It is also about religious values—the values we derive from our religious traditions and experiences such as courage, faithfulness, justice, and hope. What I have come to know and value about relationships and my responsibilities in them has come to me from two primary sources: my family and my Christian religious training. Both equipped me with information; both challenged me to think for myself. Both conveyed the collective wisdom of my community; both taught me the value of relationships and the hard work that is required to sustain them. These are the sources for my reflections.

This book is for those of us often left out of the discussion because we don't parrot an orthodox doctrine. It is for the rest of us who live in the real world and are faced everyday with hard choices in relation to those we love. It is for those of us who are willing to acknowledge the complexity and ambiguity of these choices and to engage in the hard work of discerning the right thing to do. What I mean by "right" will become clear in the following pages, but to begin with, I mean the appropriate action, the just response, that which causes least harm to self and others.

If you are comfortable living your life based on a simple, rigid set of rules which has been handed you regarding sex and relationships, don't bother to read further. If you believe that the only place for sexual intimacy is in heterosexual marriage and that whatever happens in that configuration is by definition good and right, then put this book down. It is not for you.

But if you have questions and dilemmas and have not found many people willing to help you wrestle with answers . . .

If you feel like your religious background has left you stranded with few resources to address your relational experiences . . .

If you have come to realize that a list of rules and regulations is not adequate for the situations which you face and you are looking for a way of considering your choices and evaluating your options in order to act in a way which is consistent with your values . . .

. . . then join the rest of us. This book is for you.

PART I
Establishing a Context

1 Ethics for the Rest of Us

After spending two hours presenting the introduction to a teenage sexual abuse prevention program to parents, I was asked this question by a father: "All I want to know is, are you going to tell them what's right and what's wrong?" Unprepared as I was for this particular question, I replied nonetheless, "Yes, I will tell them that it is right to share sexual intimacy in a context of choice and commitment and it is wrong to coerce, force or take advantage of anyone sexually." I doubt that I satisfied that particular parent's concern, but I was as honest as I could be.

❧ WHAT IS ETHICS? Ethics is the process of considering a choice between right and wrong, a choice which then shapes behavior. Morals is the more commonplace term and is sometimes contrasted with ethics, which is considered a more academic or abstract discussion of ideals. But I will avoid the term "moral" because it carries connotations of "moralism" which for many people describes the efforts of one group to impose its particular moral code onto others. Instead I will discuss the process of ethical discernment: the choosing of actions, the consequences of each choice, and the values which one wants to embody in her/his actions. The one exception is that I will use the term "moral agency" (which comes from the field of ethics) to describe the fact that persons have the capacity to make ethical decisions and act on them.

Rule-Based Ethics

For many people, much of traditional ethics as it was applied to personal decision making has been rule-based ethics. Someone (parents or the minister) handed down a list of rules (for example, the Ten Commandments or the Church's teaching), and the only thing that was important was that you learned the rules and followed them. If you followed the rules, you were considered a good person and your salvation was assured. If you didn't follow the rules, you were a bad person and often guilt-ridden. These rules were provided by the religious institutions ("Thou shalt not commit adultery"), the family ("Don't marry beneath you") and the community ("Premarital sex for girls is wrong"). Whatever the source, the rules reflected community norms—and usually a double standard for women and men.

Many of the rules did not make a lot of sense and the reasons given for them were confusing and inadequate. Take for example, the rule against masturbation: why should one not masturbate? Because it will give you warts on your hands. When folklore wouldn't suffice, the Bible was often invoked as the last word on the matter. Thus, we were told, because the Bible says so, it was contrary to God's procreative purpose for sex.

Or consider the rule against premarital sex: why should one not engage in genital sexual activity before marriage? Because you could get pregnant (for girls). Because you could get *her* pregnant (for boys). The real concern here was practical: pregnancy out of wedlock was stigmatized. One should avoid offending the community sensibilities if one wanted to continue to live in that community. Never mind the fact that the young woman's future was inexorably changed by her pregnancy.

Or the rule against homosexuality: both being one and behaving like one were considered sins and in many states in the United States, illegal. Why? Because it was "unnatural" and not procreative. And again, because the Bible said so.

Some rules made no sense at all and no rationale was even offered. In 1966, when our senior pastor attended the youth group discussion on sexuality (which I can assure you was quite tame), his one piece of advice was: never date anyone you wouldn't marry. Why not, I wondered? How else can you find out if this is a person you might want to marry? It was at this point that I began to question the value of unexamined rules.

The other problem with most rule-based ethics, especially sexual ethics, is that they tend to miss the point. For example, the rule that one should not engage in sexual activity outside of heterosexual marriage continues to be the foundation for the United Methodist dictum regarding ordained clergy: "Fidelity in marriage and celibacy in singleness." This rule can be used to justify all sexual activity that happens within heterosexual marriage and yet condemn all sexual activity that happens outside of heterosexual marriage, at least for clergy. Hence if a man forces a woman to have sex before they are married, this is bad and we call it rape. If he forces her to have sex two weeks after they are married, this is acceptable—as if the social status of the relationship alone indicates something about its quality. Diana Russell's finding that one in seven wives reports marital rape by their husbands would seem to indicate that the rule requiring that sexual activity take place only in heterosexual marriage is inadequate to safeguard the welfare of wives or to insure the ethical conduct of husbands. Besides, this rule was based primarily on the preservation of male property rights and was never intended to address the safety of wives.

In the late 1960s in the United States, Joseph Fletcher published a book titled *Situation Ethics*. Fletcher's thesis was that ethical decision making had to be shaped primarily by the situation in which a decision was made, rather than by the traditional rules which might apply. Predictably, he was condemned by most conservatives and praised by most liberals. The strength of Fletcher's contribution was that he relativized ethics by saying that the right choice depended more on the situation than on the rule. But his relativism was also the weakness of his effort. He relativized the discussion to the extent that there were no bottom lines, no givens, no lines that should not be crossed. Everything was dependent on the specific situation. This gave liberals abundant permission to justify just about anything; this is what made conservatives crazy.

Fletcher's necessary, but nonetheless unnerving, argument created an either/or perception. Either there are clear, rigid rules for everyone or there is nothing, no moral guide except whatever the individual can justify to her or himself. As a result, conservatives clung tightly to traditional rules and liberals floundered with no guidelines at all except an occasional facile reference to "Judge not that you not be judged."

The Creation of an Ethical Vacuum

In the early 1970s, conservatives' worst fears were realized with the emergence of so-called sexual liberation. The availability of relatively safe, affordable, trust-worthy contraception and the successes of the pro-choice movement were either nightmares or dreams come true, depending on one's perspective. Conservatives blamed relativism and secular humanism, and foretold the demise of the family and the downfall of civilization as we know it. Liberals seized upon the opportunity for "open marriage" and "sexual freedom."

But it was the gay liberation movement which posed the greatest challenge, by laying the fact of homosexuality on the table for both church and society. Up until then there had been little controversy and no real challenge to the "no sex outside of marriage" rule, even though heterosexual behavior frequently did not adhere to it. The presence of openly gay and lesbian activists calling for civil rights, and of openly gay and lesbian Christians seeking recognition and affirmation in the churches, was a wake-up call for ethicists. Simultaneously, the women's movement was helping women to name rape and other forms of sexual violence as common experiences in women's lives. But this piece of the puzzle was conveniently overlooked by churches and, to a large extent, by society in its nascent debate about sex which focused on the norm of heterosexual marriage in response to the appeals from gay and lesbian voices for recognition and acceptance. What became abundantly clear was that neither the traditional conservative nor liberal positions were adequate to help real people deal with the real issues of their sexual experiences.

Homosexuality, because it involved sex outside of marriage and because same-sex sexual activity was regarded as taboo by the dominant culture, became the focus for what is really a much larger issue of sexual ethics. But this focus has allowed both church and society to avoid the larger questions of sexual ethics which apply to heterosexuals as well as lesbians and gays: issues such as sexual abuse, prevention of sexually transmitted diseases, commitment, and sex education. For over twenty years, the argument has raged in both legislatures and church conventions: is it good for someone to be gay or lesbian and to behave like one—that is, to be sexually active? Perhaps more practically, is it tolerable within the dominant heterosexual culture? Most of the religious discussions have fallen under the heading of "human sexuality studies." Most of the actual studies which have been produced by denominational bodies have rightly brought forth research in biblical studies, theology, ethics, and the social sciences. Although these studies have concluded that there is no real basis for the condemnation of homosexuality,* denominational conventions have repeatedly rejected their own studies and continue to rationalize their condemnation of homosexuality based though it is on prejudice and homophobia. These denominations maintain the dictum of sexual activity only within heterosexual marriage as the *sine qua non* of sexual ethics and deny gays and lesbians the legal or

---

* See "Human Sexuality and the Christian Faith," Division for Church and Society, Evangelical Lutheran Church in America, November, 1991; "Report of the Committee to Study Homosexuality to the General Council of the United Methodist Church," August 24, 1991; "Keeping Body and Soul Together: Sexuality, Spirituality, and Social Justice," The 203rd General Assembly Special Committee On Human Sexuality, Presbyterian Church (U.S.A.), 1991.

ecclesiastic option of marriage, creating an intentional Catch-22 which they hope will discourage same-sex sexual activity. Then they explain that it is okay to *be* gay or lesbian (citing research evidence that some people are born this way) as long as gays and lesbians are not sexually active.

Again, the concern seems to be same-sex sexual *activity*. When the question of possible harm does arise, some still erroneously cite the belief that homosexuals are likely to molest children;[1] others argue that homosexuality destroys families. But no one seems to be able to explain how a healthy, mature, responsible gay or lesbian person causes injury to others anymore than a healthy, mature, responsible heterosexual person causes injury to others. Still, in the dominant discourse, same-sex sexual activity is viewed as deviant and unacceptable, thus establishing a double standard for sexual ethics while simultaneously sidestepping the ethical questions that a less phobic response would allow.

How is it that religious groups have spent so much time and energy on this argument? It is certainly important to those of us who are gay or lesbian, but why must we convince these institutions that we are human beings who live in families, work in communities, pay taxes, and are capable of moral agency? Of course our efforts must continue because these institutions exercise enormous power over our lives and they must be changed. But what is so appalling is that the church in particular has allowed its obsession with homosexuality to dominate its agenda year after year while virtually ignoring other pressing ethical issues like economic injustice, ecology, racism, sexual and domestic violence, and sexual ethics.

This impasse in the church on the issue of homosexuality has left an enormous vacuum. There has been substantive discussion of medical ethics in the face of new technological options and some teachers such as James Nelson have persisted in discussing sexuality in the church; valuable contributions to the discussion of sexual and relational ethics have come from feminist ethicists and theologians such as Beverly Wildung Harrison, Margaret Farley, Karen Lebacqz, and Mary Hunt, and from womanist theologians such as Toinette Eugene and Delores Williams, as well as from authors Alice Walker and Toni Morrison, to name but a few. Courageous voices such as that of Charles Curran and others within Roman Catholicism have attempted to move the discussion forward only to be censured by their church. But by and large, there has been little help from the church or the community for ordinary people living ordinary lives and facing extraordinary dilemmas. People need and deserve some assistance.* They are desperate to find ways to live their lives with some sense of ethical and spiritual congruence. Many have left the church in reaction to the rigid moralism and hypocrisy they found there. They take these questions to therapists, few of whom have been trained to deal with ethical discernment. They share their dilemmas with friends or colleagues and find that they are not alone, but they also find that no one else has an answer either.

Moral Agency

Moral agency is the human capacity to make moral choices and then to act on those choices. For example, I can choose to pay for a loaf of bread in the store (to fairly compensate the baker for her materials and labor) or to pick it up and walk out without paying. After making that choice to pay for the bread, then I can act based on the choice. Granted there may be multiple motivations for my choice, not the least of which is my awareness of the consequences of getting caught for shoplifting, but I still am exercising moral agency when I pay for the bread.

---

* The denominational studies mentioned earlier were a valiant attempt to address important issues and to bring a healthy discussion of human sexuality to the laity. In addition, there are curricula which are valuable resources for study and discussion such as *Created in God's Image: A Human Sexuality Program for Ministry and Mission* and *Affirming Persons—Saving Lives: AIDS Awareness and Prevention Education*, both from the United Church of Christ (USA); and other publications such as "The Bible and Human Sexuality," in *American Baptist Quarterly* (Dec. 1993): XII/4. Sylvia Thorson-Smith, *Reconciling the Broken Silence: The Church in Dialogue on Gay and Lesbian Issues* (Louisville, KY: Presbyterian Church [U.S.A.], 1993).

It is often assumed that each of us comes to an ethical decision with equal awareness and resources with which to exercise our moral agency. This is not the case. In fact we each bring our own particularity to the process of ethical decision making, a fact often overlooked by traditional, rule-based ethics. Our particularity includes our social status as a function of gender, race, class, sexual orientation, age, and physical ability. For some of us, it includes experiences of privilege which present options upon which a general model of ethical decision making is based. My payment to the baker for the bread she has baked is an option because I have money with which to pay. I have not only the capacity of character but the material means to exercise moral agency in that particular situation. For many others, our particularity includes our experiences of discrimination or oppression and possibly of victimization, all of which impact our decision making. For example, for an adult woman who experienced sexual abuse throughout childhood and adolescence and who through that experience comes to learn that she has no choice about what happens to her own body, the very notion of "choice" is foreign. Judith Herman explains:

> [R]epeated abuse . . . is passively experienced as a dreaded but unavoidable fate and is accepted as the inevitable price of relationship. Many survivors have such profound deficiencies in self-protection that they can barely imagine themselves in a position of agency or choice. The idea of saying no to the emotional demands of a parent, spouse, lover, or authority figure may be practically inconceivable.[2]

Previous experiences of abuse profoundly shape an individual's perception of "normality" and of what is ethically acceptable.

> Rosemary was sexually assaulted in her first marriage 30 years ago; she commented about her second marriage: "And I suppose I just really didn't know, I thought that was normal, [my husband having sex with me] seven or eight or ten times a night, and through the day, and I was pregnant. . . . [I] just couldn't

understand why I couldn't . . . get any pleasure out of being with him, and why it was so painful. You know, why people talked about it as being so wonderful, and why, for me, it was just absolute agony."[3]

This distortion of "normality" is common for anyone whose earliest sexual experiences were coercive. Sex becomes equated with something that someone else does to you, not something about which you have any choice. When this experience is juxtaposed with the images of romance which abound in music, soap operas, and films, the results can be very confusing. As Rosemary said, everyone talked about sex being so wonderful; for her it was agony. The result is isolation, confusion, and lack of awareness of the potential for choice or moral agency.

Ironically, it is often those who have experienced chronic abuse who are most concerned with questions of moral choice, guilt, and responsibility. At a workshop entitled "Sex, Power and Choice," the primary concern for participants who were abuse survivors was trying to understand how they had "consented" to years of abuse and exploitation. They said things like, "But I let him do this to me for years," and "I should have known better, I guess." Although this may seem to be only another version of the self-blame that is common for survivors of abuse, their struggle to understand consent was an indicator of their desire to exercise genuine moral agency and make their own choices. They came from experiences of abuse where they were denied authentic consent (the right to say "no" and have that "no" respected). Yet they were simultaneously told by their abuser that they were consenting, that this experience was chosen by them: "Sure, you can go or stay anytime you want to. But if you break up with me, just remember, no one else will have you; everyone knows you're a slut anyway." Thus they felt responsible for choosing to stay even after they had begun to see that it was harmful to them. This contradiction is what Judith Herman labels "doublethink." It is a method frequently employed by an abuser to control the victim by denying her/him any possibility of genuine moral agency. Victims/survivors are susceptible to the belief that they are consenting because this belief allows them to feel that they are not totally powerless. But it overlooks the fact that their capacity for moral agency has been significantly compromised by their circumstance and by the coercion of the abuser. This is perhaps the cruelest of frauds perpetrated by an abuser.

Moral agency requires that we possess power and resources (see chapter 3, "Power, Boundaries, and Common Sense"). We must have knowledge and awareness in order to exercise sound judgment. We cannot exercise choice if we do not have options and the ability to act. Anything which denies or compromises these resources undercuts moral agency.

This is not to suggest that even in circumstances where one's ability to act as moral agent is compromised that one still cannot exercise moral agency. Moral agency can be carried out against the greatest of odds. However to do so, one must be able to see through the charade which is being attempted by the person with greater power. And one must be willing and able to accept the consequences, which may include punishment, economic loss, or loss of relationship. Moral agency does not come without cost, but if one's exercise of moral agency in a relationship (choosing to say "no" to a sexual overture, for example) leads to the loss of that relationship, it is a sure indicator that the relationship was not one of mutual respect and authentic consent in the first place.

On the other hand, sometimes those who have the capacity and resources to exercise moral agency attempt to deny their ability in order to avoid responsibility for their actions. The father who explained that his daughter came up to him and unzipped his pants and "What else was I supposed to do?" in order to justify his sexual abuse of this four-year old child was denying that he had power and responsibility. He refused to acknowledge that his response to her should have been to zip up his pants and leave her unmolested. It is a paradox how often those who have the most resources and opportunity to exercise moral agency seek to deny it. Likewise, those who have the least opportunity to exercise moral agency seek to assume it. For example, as the woman beaten by her partner with a baseball bat stated: "I should have stopped him; I should never have said anything about his drinking; it only upsets him." All too often those who have responsibility in a situation deny it, and those who do not have responsibility claim that they do.

In this book, I will assume that the reader is seeking ways to exercise her/his moral agency in matters of intimate relationships. But this book also recognizes the multitudes of ways in which our ability to act as moral agents is compromised. We all live in the tension between the possibility of moral choice and the actuality of its limitations, especially those of us who, through accident of birth, find ourselves on the underside of socially constructed reality (see chapter 3, "Power, Boundaries and Common Sense"). This book will seek to empower those whose moral choices have been limited by increasing their awareness and understanding, and to challenge those who have traditionally had more options to exercise those options responsibly. It will argue for an ethic of sexual justice which, according to John Stoltenberg, involves "determining to learn as much as one can know about the values in the acts one has done and the acts one chooses to do and their full consequences for other people—as if everyone else is absolutely as real as oneself."[4]

So We Proceed

This book is not about sexuality, a topic far beyond the scope of my efforts here. It is about intimate relationships and sexual ethics, and about the dilemmas we face every day about sexual activity and intimacy in relationships.

This book will not be definitive; I will not address every ethical issue that arises in relationships. I will not suggest a new list of rules to follow. But neither will I be situational and relativistic. I take a clear position on a number of issues. I will suggest specific guidelines for decision making, and I will share the wisdom which others have discovered in their discernment processes. I will not give you easy answers or make decisions for you.

I have divided the book into two parts. Part I, "Establishing a Context," provides the necessary background for this discussion including what I mean by "ethics," why I use "doing least harm" as an ethical standard, what power has to do with all this, and what particular issues face heterosexual men and women. In Part II, "Guidelines for Relationships," I offer five specific guidelines to help guide one's ethical discernment and actions.

I have chosen to use different voices in the text: Sometimes I speak singularly in the first person about my own experiences. Sometimes I speak generally and the "we" which I mean is usually apparent: at times it refers to the common experiences of women; at others, to the common experiences of women and men. Sometimes I speak to you, the reader, in the second person. Sometimes I speak about women and men in the third person. Pay attention to these differences; I think you will find that some of your assumptions about gender or sexual orientation will be challenged in the process. I am trying to speak to our experiences, yours and mine, without assuming that they are always the same or even similar, without assuming that they are in any way necessarily universal, and yet trying to find the points where you, the reader, may be able to say, "Yes, I know about that."

I will use various references and sources throughout, including biblical and academic references. For some of you, the biblical references may seem jarring and you may feel some resistance to them, for example my use of Paul's writings from Christian scripture. For others, these may be reassuring and may resonate with your own use of biblical material. I have chosen the sources which have been most useful to me and which I therefore value in my own discernment process and seek to share here in regard to practical issues. I urge you to listen carefully to these sources; you may be surprised to find some words of wisdom which speak to your experience.

There are four assumptions which precede this entire discussion:

1. Most people live in relationships of varying degrees of intimacy and most would prefer to do this with integrity.

2. Both women and men are moral agents and both possess the capacity and responsibility for ethical decision making and action. Our perceptions of our options are likely to be shaped by our gender, race, age, class, and sexual orientation, and are likely to be different because of our experiences. But we share capacity and responsibility regardless of who we are.

3. No particular gender or relational configuration is assumed. This book attempts to speak to all persons— regardless of sexual orientation or relational configuration—who are looking for guidance in relationships. Likewise "family" refers to those persons with whom one chooses to live in a committed relationship (which may involve providing care to those who are vulnerable due to age, disability, or infirmity).

4. Healthy intimate relationships are possible only in the open, and in community. Secrecy encourages shame and isolation which make it very difficult to discern ethical choices. On the other hand, privacy is necessary to provide the time and space for a relationship to know intimacy. The challenging task in an intimate relationship is to find the delicate balance between privacy and public life which supports the relationship.

Finally this entire discussion of sexual ethics is grounded in an incarnational theology. "Incarnational theology" is an academic term which refers to a theology which affirms the body as a good gift from God and the wholeness of self, meaning that one relates to self, others, and the world physically, emotionally, and spiritually. We experience the presence of God moving within and among us as the force of life itself. For example, there are many moments of connection between persons in which our fullest presence is shared with another, in which the physical, emotional, and spiritual are manifest simultaneously in an experience which can be life-giving and just: the moment that the caring surgeon's knife pierces the flesh of the patient with the singular purpose of relieving suffering and bringing healing; the mother nursing her child; the release from prison of a person who was unjustly incarcerated and for whom a group has worked to win her release; the father watching and assisting his partner as their child is born; the adult, once illiterate, now reading a poem to his teacher; the celebration of the end of apartheid on the part of all of those who helped bring it to an end; the adult daughter helping to bathe her own mother incapacitated by illness; a deep, wet kiss with one's intimate partner; the memorial of the AIDS Quilt not only for what it represents, but for the loving hands that made it. For me, incarnational theology acknowledges God's presence in everyday experiences such as these.

God as the fundamental source of our being is present in each of these experiences. But none of these experiences *necessarily* manifests a love that does no harm; hence the need for ethical questions. For some people, these particular experiences might in fact be harmful. But moments such as these contain *the possibility* of love doing no harm, of love making justice. It is not the act itself but rather the quality and conditions of the relationship which determine the actuality of love and justice in relationship. Jesus taught that God wills for us abundance of life, which I believe means that God wills for us to know love and justice in relationship with others. This discussion of sexual ethics rests within this understanding of incarnational theology and ethics.

The process of ethical discernment is the way that we can bring our head and our heart to the sometimes complex choices which face us in an intimate relationship. To discern is to figure out, sort through, or consider options and consequences. To discern ethically is to consider options, evaluate them based on our values, make a choice and act on that choice. If we love ourselves and the other with whom we are engaging, if we want to do them no harm, then the time and energy we spend in ethical discernment will be well worth the investment.

2 Doing Least Harm

What matters is the center inside yourself—and how you live, and how you treat people, and what you can contribute as you pass through life on this earth, and how honestly you love, and how carefully you make choices. Those are the things that really matter.

—John Stoltenberg, *Refusing to Be a Man*

WE COULD BEGIN a discussion of ethical choices in relationships by positing a vision of a just relationship and working back from there. For this we need models to guide us. This is the approach which Mary Hunt takes in her critically acclaimed book, *Fierce Tenderness: a Theology of Friendship.* Hunt argues that marriage is neither the most common nor the most useful model for relationship, but that friendship is. Everyone knows something about friendship and has experienced the joy and the pain it brings. The values and expectations which we bring to friendship can and should shape our significant relationships, whether they are more or less intimate.

A Place To Begin

Given that friendship is an excellent precursor to a good sexual relationship, I want to discuss the very concrete ethical questions which confront an intimate relationship. How do we do it everyday? How do we make real a commitment to equality, respect, love, and justice in our most significant relationships?

I start from what may sound like a negative place: doing least harm.* Why not "doing most good" or "making justice," you may well ask? "Doing most good" and "making justice" are the vision of possibility for which we may strive in relationship. But "doing least harm" is probably what we are capable of. Doing least harm is a realistic and tangible goal to set for ourselves. I may not know what is the most good that I could do, and if I know, I may not be capable of it. But I probably have an idea about the harm that I could do and hopefully am capable of avoiding it. Avoiding harm is also one of the oldest stated ethical expectations for those in the helping professions. The Hippocratic Oath (fifth century BCE) requires physicians to "keep [patients] from harm and injustice."[1] This simple and profound expectation is essential to love making justice in any relationship.

The most important reason to begin here is that doing least harm is a fundamental and concrete ethical principle. "How do I avoid doing harm to myself and to another?" should be the first question we ask when we are considering our own actions. It pushes us to consider the impact of our behavior on ourselves and on others. In perhaps the apostle Paul's most significant contribution to ethics, he brings together the teachings of Judaism and Christianity and focuses an ethical mandate:

> Owe no one anything except to love one another; for the one who loves another has fulfilled the law. The commandments, "You shall not commit adultery; You shall not murder; You shall not steal; You shall not covet;" and any other command- ment, are summed up in this word, "Love your neighbor as yourself." Love does no wrong to a neighbor; therefore, love is the fulfilling of the law. (Romans 13:8–10 NRSV).

Love does no harm to another. If I am seeking to love another person, I can best begin by trying not to do harm to that person. Love your neighbor as yourself. Self-love is necessary if I am to

---

* This is the title of a poem written in 1983 by Jody Aliesan.

ever love another person. These mandates represent the foundation for any viable sexual ethics.

While my suggestion of a distinction between love and harm may seem self-evident to the reader, I would argue that it is not. The endemic problems of sexual and domestic violence inflicted primarily in intimate, family relationships would suggest that in some perverse way, "love" and harm have become equated. Contemporary music and films persist in the message that sex is violent and violence is sexy. Batterers commonly explain their violence towards their partners as a manifestation of their love: "I guess I just loved her too much to let her go." Or, they distort love's meaning by inverted logic: "I love her therefore whatever I do to her is out of love and cannot be harmful" and justify whatever means they employ to control her. Women sometimes rationalize staying with an abusive partner because they love him.

Harm is that which inflicts physical pain, damage or injury and/or diminishes the other person's dignity and self-worth. (Harm is not the distress experienced by an abusive partner when he is arrested and held accountable for assaulting his partner.) Love is a passionate, affectionate desire characterized by genuine concern for the well-being of the other. The line between love and harm has become blurred. The two should not be confused nor collapsed. They are contradictory—hence the assertion "love does no harm."

But what about love of self and doing least harm to one's self? How do we fulfill this ethical mandate as well in an intimate relationship? This is an issue for women to consider in particular, because we have been taught to give up concern for ourselves in an intimate relationship. We have been poured out to meet the needs of others. We have been too much concerned with others and too little concerned for ourselves. Consequently, we have been easily taken advantage of in relationships. On the other hand, self-love is not to be confused with self-centeredness or selfishness, that is, concern for self above all others. This selfishness is the temptation for some people who disregard the needs of others in order to meet their own needs (which is usually the case for abusers).

If love of self precedes love of another, then doing least harm to self should also precede doing least harm to another. Practically speaking, this means having self-respect and expecting to be treated with respect by one's partner. It means walking away from a relationship with someone who is clearly not concerned for your well-being. Now all of this is easier said than done. There are many women, for example, who have tried to walk away from an abusive relationship only to be pursued, injured, or killed. There are people who have said "no, thank you" to a sexual overture only to be stalked and harassed. Although the principle of doing least harm sounds fine, the practical implications of doing least harm can get very complicated. For example, if a woman and her children are repeatedly abused by her partner, if she has been unsuccessful in getting away, does she not have the right to defend herself by force? In this situation, doing least harm to herself and her children—that is, trying to protect herself and the children from harm—takes precedence. She is faced with the difficulty of finding her options limited because of the harm she is suffering at the hands of her partner. It is not always easy to find the way to do least harm to oneself and to another person in an intimate relationship.

Beginning with "doing least harm" as a primary ethical principle provides a point of reference for ethical discernment. Does what I am doing cause harm to my neighbor/friend/intimate or to myself? If we apply this standard to the ethical questions raised in the first chapter, we can see why the answers of rule-based ethics are inadequate while those based on the principle of "doing least harm" allow for reasonable ethical discernment.

- Does masturbation cause harm to anyone? Not in and of itself. Like any other human activity, it can be misused and thus harm oneself or one's partner.
- Does premarital sex cause harm to anyone? Not in and of itself. But like any sexual activity, premarital sex could

harm another if it is not authentically consensual, is not done with full knowledge, does not include protection against pregnancy and disease, and is not engaged in by two persons who are emotionally and psychologically mature and are peers to one another.

- Does homosexuality cause harm to anyone? Not in and of itself any more than does heterosexuality. Any sexual relationship has the potential to do harm to self or to another regardless of the genders of the persons involved. But lesbians, gays, bisexuals, and heterosexuals have the capacity to engage in relationships which embody love, care, equality, respect, justice, etc.

- Does dating someone you would not marry cause harm to anyone? I don't think so.

Doing least harm is a practical and reasonable standard. It makes sense that we would strive not to harm another or ourselves because the consequences of harm are painful and destructive. Therefore doing least harm can be a useful starting point for our efforts at ethical discernment in intimate relationships.

Guidelines

If doing least harm is our goal in relationship to others, what guidelines might assist us?

Guidelines allow us to be particular about the values we bring to our effort to do least harm. They provide a framework within which to make daily choices in a relationship. In order to work, they must be reasonable and thus reasonably follow from the principle of doing least harm. As such, they also provide a short cut to decision making. Once we have arrived at guidelines which reflect our original principle, we can refer to them quickly in our discernment process and make our choices more readily. The development of guidelines is an ongoing process, and is best carried out together with others in community so that we can test our own ideas against their experiences and concerns.

What is the difference between guidelines and rules? Rules are externally imposed requirements which may or may not have a reasonable basis. They sometimes represent the common concerns (or prejudices) of society and are usually expressed in legal statutes or codes of ethics enacted by some representative body such as a state legislature. They may be necessary to sustain the common good and protect those who are vulnerable (for example marital rape laws), or they may be counterproductive (such as sodomy laws). But rules and laws are not adequate to guide our actions as moral agents and decision makers within our significant relationships. The guidelines which I am suggesting here are standards by which you can determine your choices and actions. They are an internal anchor which can inform your decision-making.

These particular guidelines or parameters are useful when applied to intimate, sexual relationships. I believe they are necessary in order to do least harm in such a relationship.

1. Is my choice of intimate partner a peer, that is, someone whose power is relatively equal to mine? We must limit our sexual interaction to our peers and recognize that those who are vulnerable to us, that is, who have less power than we do, are off limits for our sexual interests.

2. Are both my partner and I authentically consenting to our sexual interaction? Both of us must have information, awareness, equal power, and the option to say "no" without being punished as well as the option to say "yes."

3. Do I take responsibility for protecting myself and my partner against sexually-transmitted diseases and to insure reproductive choice? This is a question of stewardship (the wise care for and management of the gift of sexuality) and anticipating the literal consequences of our actions. Taking this responsibility seriously presupposes a relationship: knowing someone over time and sharing a history in which trust can develop.

4. Am I committed to sharing sexual pleasure and intimacy in my relationship? My concern should be both for my own needs and those of my partner.

5. Am I faithful to my promises and commitments? Whatever the nature of a commitment to one's partner and whatever the duration of that commitment, fidelity requires honesty and the keeping of promises. Change in an individual may require a change in the commitment which hopefully can be achieved through open and honest communication.

Each of these guidelines will be discussed in its own chapter. I offer them because I believe that if we use these guidelines to inform our ethical choices, we end up insuring that we do not meet our own sexual needs at the expense of another person. Surely this takes us a long way toward doing least harm to that person, to ourselves and toward living in a just relationship in which trust and intimacy can thrive.

Before we can discuss these guidelines, we should consider the way that power in relationships impacts an ethical discussion. The critical, and oftentimes complicated, issue of power is always a factor for better or for worse in our intimate relationships. In conjunction with the discussion of power, we will also examine the particular ways that issues of power affect heterosexuals who are struggling with ethical discernment in intimate relationships.

3 Power, Boundaries, and Common Sense

Power is a basic human reality because we are related to each other. However, our conventional understandings of power are colored by our experiences of life in societies of male dominance. From those experiences we come to believe that power is hierarchical and is demonstrated by dominance, by status, by authority, and by control over people, nature, and things. This may be the power we know, but it is not the power we were born with.

The fundamental power of life, born into us, heals, makes whole, empowers, and liberates. Its manifold forms create and emerge from heart, that graceful, passionate mystery at the center of ourselves and each other. This power heals brokenheartedness and gives courage to the fainthearted.

—Rita Nakashima Brock, *Journeys by Heart*

The word *lover*, purged of romantic-sentimental associations, becomes a name for what human beings might mean to each other in a world where each person held both power and responsibility.

—Adrienne Rich, "Power and Danger: Works of a Common Woman"

ANY DISCUSSION OF SEXUAL ETHICS at this point in time must acknowledge the context of power and the issues it raises. Power and the lack of it are influential, yet often unacknowledged factors in any intimate relationship. Power must be addressed before options and decision making in intimate relationships can be considered. Along with power, we must consider boundaries. How do we understand the limits that give shape to our relationships? How do we respect another's boundaries as we develop and live out a relationship? How do we communicate our own? Hopefully this discussion comes full circle to common sense, that is, common sense which arises from a desire for just relationships. This common sense can then inform our process of ethical discernment and decision making.

Power

Most simply, power is the capacity to act; this capacity requires resources. I cannot teach mathematics (act) unless I have knowledge of mathematics and the skill to teach it (resources). Resources can be material or non-material: money and ownership of property is a resource but so is knowledge, self-confidence, and status or role. Power is essentially neutral: it is neither good nor bad in itself. Its moral quality is determined by the use to which we put it.

As children we learn very early on that our parents have power, and that they can use that power to protect us, provide for our needs, discipline and teach us—or abuse us. We also learn that the sources of their power are their role as parents, their age, and their physical size vis-à-vis us as children. The distribution of power among human beings is largely socially constructed which means that it is also somewhat arbitrary.* So within a patriarchal culture, for example, men have determined that they have more power than women and they act accordingly. The primary paradigm is that of dominance and submission which is projected onto relationships between men and women, that is, men being dominant

---

* "Social construction" means that the norms and expectations for men and women and relationships are created (constructed) by those within our social context who have the greatest power. For example, inequality is constructed by those who want to retain greater power at the expense of others and is based not only on gender but also on race, class, and sexual orientation. These factors also multiply the consequences for those deemed less than equal by those with greatest power.

and women being submissive. Many people in western societies have come to accept the patriarchal paradigm as normative, even as ordained by God. But there are nonpatriarchal cultures in which the idea and the behaviors of male dominance over women are quite peculiar.[1]

The absence of power, i.e. powerlessness, or lacking the capacity to act, results from a lack of resources (material and non-material). I am powerless to cross the lake if I don't have a boat; I am powerless to successfully remove a brain tumor if I am not a neurosurgeon; I am powerless to avoid being raped if I am confronted by a rapist who has a weapon and has decided to rape me, if I have no weapon or assistance from outside resources. My powerlessness or lack of resources means that I am vulnerable,* that is, I can be "physically wounded," or I am "open to attack or damage."[2] Because I am vulnerable, I can be victimized, that is, I can be "killed, destroyed, injured or otherwise harmed by . . . some act, condition, agency or circumstance."[3]

These conditions—having power, being powerless, being vulnerable, being victimized—are common to all human beings depending on a variety of circumstances that may occur at any moment in our lives. None of these conditions is absolute in human experience. We never have absolute power with no vulnerability, nor do we ever have absolute vulnerability with no resources (except perhaps at the moment of our death). We have more or less power and greater or fewer resources. We are more or less vulnerable.

This reality of our powerlessness or vulnerability does not sit well with us humans. We don't like the fact that under some circumstances we do not possess the resources to protect ourselves, that we can be victimized, and that we may not survive; hence our longing for power and resources. We believe that we can insure against vulnerability if we have power and resources. This

---

* In contemporary psychobabble, "vulnerable" is often used to describe a feeling of emotional openness and is valued positively. This use of the term clouds the word's meaning which is more accurately tied to lack of power and resources.

is why the superpowers engaged in the arms race for decades. This is why many men and women now carry firearms believing that this resource will lessen their vulnerability to assault.

Some of us, because of our social positioning or circumstance, will never have adequate power and resources to negate our vulnerability and insure against our being victimized. Children are *by definition* vulnerable human beings. This is why it is so difficult to stop child sexual abuse. We can increase a child's resources through education, which lessens the child's vulnerability somewhat, but we cannot change the fact that children are physically smaller than adults and dependent upon them. Aging also brings about physical vulnerability. Illness or physical disability make us vulnerable no matter who we are. The president of the United States possesses extraordinary power and resources. But if he is lying on the operating table for open heart surgery, he is as vulnerable as any other patient—his only advantage is that he probably has access to better health care than any other patient. In a patriarchal culture, women by definition, and as a class, have fewer resources than men and hence are more vulnerable. For example, women in the United States still make between sixty and seventy cents for every dollar that men make. Similarly, racial minorities in a majority culture have less access to resources (unless steps have been taken to insure equity) and as such are vulnerable. To use a mundane example: in Hong Kong, my traveling companion who was African-American stepped out to hail a taxi. Several empty cabs passed her by. When she stepped back and I stepped forward, the first one who saw me stopped because I was white. I had access to a resource that was denied her because she was African-American. Racism determined the distribution of resources available to us. These are very real experiences of power and powerlessness which are operative in every relationship and every interaction between human beings. Like it or not, all of us experience power *and* vulnerability at various points in our lives.

What do we do about these facts of life? The Hebrew people recognized that these realities posed a fundamental ethical question:

How should we relate to vulnerability, both others' and our own? Recognizing that lacking resources and being vulnerable are undeniable human experiences, how should those who have resources and are less vulnerable at any one time relate to those who are more vulnerable? Their answer was the hospitality code. At several points in Hebrew Scripture the expectation is clearly stated: "For the Lord your God is . . . the great God . . . who executes justice for the orphan and the widow, and who loves the strangers, providing them food and clothing. You shall also love the stranger . . ." And why this directive? ". . . for you were strangers in the land of Egypt" (Deuteronomy 10:17–19 NRSV; see also Leviticus 19:33–34; Exodus 22:21–24). The expectation is repeated over and over in scripture: "Give justice to the weak and the orphan; maintain the right of the lowly and the destitute. Rescue the weak and the needy; deliver them from the hand of the wicked" (Psalm 82:3–4 NRSV; see also Isaiah 1:16–17 and 10:1–2). Whom does scripture identify as those whom we are to protect, support, and treat justly? Those who have the least resources by virtue of their social status and circumstance, and are therefore vulnerable: widows, orphans, the weak, the needy, and strangers, or travelers. Why should we be concerned for them? Because we have also been in that position of vulnerability; we know what it feels like to be without resources, and we could be in that position again at any moment. For example, if you have ever traveled in a country where you did not speak or read the language, you know how it feels to be vulnerable. In that situation, you are dependent on the goodwill of those around you, whether you like it or not.

Being vulnerable or having fewer resources in and of itself is not a bad thing. It does not predict that we will necessarily be harmed or injured. The fact of our vulnerability only becomes a problem if those around us seek to take advantage of it and do us harm. If rather than protecting us, as the hospitality code encourages them to do, they view a vulnerable person as an opportunity to exploit, then our vulnerability may well result in our injury. But if an adult, for example, understands that he has more power than a child and that his power is to be used to protect that child and provide for her needs, then she will not be harmed by him. Her vulnerability and his power will not result in her exploitation or injury. His task as a responsible adult is to provide her the resources, education, and support necessary for her to learn to protect herself as she grows and develops: that is, to empower her and to encourage her to use her resources to protect others who may be vulnerable.

In recent years we have seen both the denial of power (on the part of those who have more resources) and denial of vulnerability (on the part of those who have fewer resources) as part of a backlash against the efforts of many who have been naming the reality of the victimization of women and children. One of the ways that those who do choose to take advantage of others' vulnerabilities then try to hide their actions from view is to deny that they have power or use power at all. This way, they reason, they cannot be held accountable for their misuse of power. They assert that the other person (whom they took advantage of) was not in fact vulnerable at all, but had abundant resources: "I'm just her therapist. I don't have any power here at all. If anything, she has all the power." Or they argue that there was no harm, no injury as a result of their misuse of power. So we hear from an incestuous father: "It's nobody's business. Didn't do her any harm. I mean, she never said she didn't like it. Besides, better that I teach her about sex than some pimply faced boy who doesn't know anything."

On the other hand, those of us who are most often vulnerable, who lack power and resources, may also deny our vulnerability and lack of resources as a way of bolstering our confidence and carrying on—in spite of the reality of our vulnerability. This is the "whistling in the dark" strategy. For victims, the denial of reality can be the acceptance of fate: "Well, it wasn't rape, you know. It didn't really hurt; he got what he wanted and then he left me alone. Besides, that's just the way men are." Or "I'm tired of always hearing women talked about as victims. I'm no victim. I can take care of myself. Why are all these women whining all the time?"

It's true that not all women are victims, but this is often no more than a matter of luck. It's also true that we are not all powerless and that none of us is absolutely powerless. If we were, we would not have survived this long. We do have power and resources, more or less, depending on several factors. If we are smart, we use those resources to lessen our vulnerability. But that doesn't change the fact that as women we are vulnerable by virtue of gender in a society in which gender inequity is the order of the day. Saying it isn't so is not social change; it is understandable wishful thinking, but it doesn't make the reality of our vulnerability go away.

So what does all this have to do with sexual ethics and relationships? A lot. These realities of power and vulnerability are constant themes in our intimate relationships. As such, they affect fundamental ethical questions at every turn. It is naive to consider questions of intimacy and relationships without taking into account the realities of power and vulnerability. For example, these realities determine the possibility of authentic consent within an intimate relationship (see chapter 6, "Authentic Consent"). Authentic consent is only possible in a peer relationship where both partners have relatively equal power and resources (see chapter 5, "Choosing Peer Relationships").

As we consider these experiences of power and vulnerability in the context of sexual interaction, how do we determine the difference between "making love" and "being raped"? In late twentieth-century western culture, this question becomes more and more difficult to answer depending on one's reference point. If we look to mainstream media or pornography, there is no clear difference: violence is sexy and good sex is violent. The dominant/submissive model is the consistent theme. If we consult the experience of many women and some men, there is much confusion: often sex is something that is done to them by someone else. Just because genitals are involved doesn't tell us anything about the qualitative nature of the sexual experience.

The confusion between sexual activity and sexual violence has haunted mental health providers, the courts, and our religious institutions for generations. Because it has seemed so difficult to distinguish between the two, we have struggled with the unfortunate consequence of blaming the victim and not holding the sexual assailant accountable. If rape is only "sex that got out of control," then she must have caused it by the way she dressed, talked, or walked, and so he couldn't help himself. Boys, after all, will be boys. It is through this illogical reasoning that the victim, not the assailant, is held responsible for the fact that she is bruised, bleeding, possibly pregnant, and possibly infected with a sexually-transmitted disease. Since the assailant is seldom held accountable, his behavior is reinforced and probably repeated.

If we are to find our way out of this labyrinth, and if we are to consider seriously the ethical issues which reside here, we must begin by distinguishing between sexual violence and sexual activity, and by challenging the dominant/submissive model of intimate relationship. The one factor which most clearly determines the difference between rape and making love is consent: genuine consent is not to be confused with acquiescence, submission, or going along in order to avoid an argument. Genuine consent is possible where power is equally shared between partners. To be sure, in sexual activity there is initiating and receiving between partners, there is playful interchange, there is passion, there is exploration of new interests, *and* there is a trust between the two people for whom "no" means no, "yes" means yes, and "maybe" means maybe. But this is very different in the experience of both persons than force, coercion, or manipulation—no matter how subtle or stylized.

Challenging the dominant/submissive model of relationship is not easy. This model is promoted and reinforced at every turn. Its promoters argue that without the difference in power between one who is dominant and one who is submissive, there is no erotic energy (see chapter 4, "Particularities of Heterosexual Relationships"). The extreme manifestation of this philosophy is sadomasochism. But even it is not so extreme when compared to mainstream dominant/submissive images. Lesbian feminist writer Audre Lorde is clear and to the point in her critique:

> Sadomasochism is an institutionalized celebration of dominant/submissive relationships. And, it *prepares* us either to accept subordination or to enforce dominance. *Even in play*, to affirm that the exertion of power over powerlessness is erotic, is empowering, is to set the emotional and social stage for the continuation of that relationship, politically, socially and economically. Sadomasochism feeds the belief that domination is inevitable.[4]

Lorde reminds us that what we do in the privacy of the bedroom has implications for our life in community and vice versa. Only through the affirmation of the eroticism of equality can we seriously address the widespread acceptance of the dominant/submissive model. To promote the eroticization of equality is to deny that domination in the private or public spheres is inevitable. This is one of our ethical tasks.

"Lust" is the urge to possess or dominate sexually. Unfortunately lust is the primary script for the dominant/submissive model for sexual interaction in contemporary society. Some people use "lust" as their excuse for initiating sexual contact with an unwilling or uninterested partner. They would argue that "lust" is strong sexual passion and desire which they cannot control. (This is the common excuse used by men who ascribe to the adage "Men can't help themselves.") A man is a moral agent, and although he may not be able to control his erection, he certainly can control what he does with it. Regardless of how we understand the concept of "lust," we are still in control of any act which might come of these desires.

Lust, as it is discussed in Christian Scripture, is not merely sexual desire for another person though it is often interpreted this way.[5] In Matthew, Jesus connects "lust" with "adultery" and expands the ethical question beyond the act to the thought which precedes it: "But I say to you that everyone who looks at a woman with lust has already committed adultery with her in his heart" (Matthew 5:28

NRSV). Jesus is suggesting that the desire to commit a particular act is as significant as the act itself and that we are accountable for both. The traditional interpretation of this passage has focused on promiscuity and adultery, suggesting that any man who has sexual feelings for a woman to whom he is not married is as guilty as if he had had sex with her.* But this interpretation is too narrow.

In fact, "lust" can best be described as the desire to sexually possess or dominate another person. So Jesus' point might be more accurately expressed: "Anyone who desires in his heart to sexually possess or dominate a woman has already taken possession of her or stolen her." Augustine echoes this understanding of "lust": "The evil of lust, a name which is given to many vices, but is properly attributable to violent sexual appetite."⁶ So "lust," the exercise of power *over* another person in a sexual context, whether in thought or in deed, is unacceptable.

Sexual feelings should not be equated with "lust." To feel attraction to or desire for another person is natural and good. God created us as sexual beings with sexual needs and interests. Feeling aroused when we are around someone to whom we are attracted is not unusual, *and* we always have a choice about acting on our feelings and desires. We might have sexual feelings when bathing a child but choose not to act on those feelings with the child because we have no desire to take advantage of or to harm the child. We always have options before us and choices to make. If we accept that we are moral agents with choices and affirm the context of shared power and equality for sexual sharing, then lust will not enter into our sexual repertoire.

Boundaries

We need boundaries in every relationship. Fundamentally, boundaries are the way that I know where I stop and you begin. Trying to

---

* "Adultery" in Hebrew Scripture was used to describe multiple sexual offenses including rape and promiscuity. This is because adultery fundamentally referred to the violation of the husband's property rights. See chapter 9, "Faithfulness."

live in a relationship without boundaries is like trying to drive down the freeway with your eyes closed in a snow storm. Lots of people can get hurt. There are boundaries in both the public and private spheres. Whether it is the Bill of Rights in the United States Constitution setting out boundaries for the government, the posted speed limit on the highway, the policy stating that there can be no prayer in public schools, or the understanding that it is inappropriate for a boss to ask an employee to pick up his laundry, boundaries are necessary in public settings to establish parameters within which we can try to co-exist.

The boundaries which have the most immediate impact on our individual lives are boundaries which delineate the physical contact between us. Touch boundaries reflect both personal preferences and collective expectations, both of which are culturally shaped. Two individuals may choose to walk together holding hands which is acceptable in Western culture unless those two persons happen to be male. Then it is not accepted—or safe—in public because of the prejudice of homophobia. But in China, two men holding hands is perfectly acceptable; a man and a woman doing the same thing is not.

When we receive a touch from another person, we experience it in one of three ways. The touch may feel good and safe and make us feel good about ourselves: it may be a parent's hand on our forehead checking our temperature or a partner's rubbing our sore back. Or the touch may feel bad or painful and make us feel afraid, such as a switching from a grandparent or a slap from a partner. Or the touch may feel confusing, uncomfortable; not necessarily painful, but unsettling: such as genital stimulation by an uncle or wrestling with an older sibling which is fun until suddenly it isn't anymore.

It is not the nature of the touch itself which determines how we experience it. A kiss on the lips from a date may be wonderful; a kiss on the lips from grandma may be less so. Choice is above all what determines how we experience a particular touch from someone: Do we choose to receive it? Do we have the option to say "no thank you"? Having a choice presumes having the power to determine our touch boundaries.

This is why it is so important to teach children that they have physical boundaries and that they have real choices about them. If my nephew doesn't want to kiss me good-bye today, he doesn't have to. Next week he may feel differently. Even though he is a child (and has less power than I do as an adult), I should respect his choice about touch boundaries. It is an important lesson that will serve him well as he develops his sense of himself and his boundaries.

I recall a minister in a workshop telling a story about his family. He and his wife had been very conscientious to teach their children positive attitudes about their bodies and about sexuality. They did not want their children to grow up with negative feelings as they had. So one of the ways the parents sought to instill positive body messages was not to wear clothing to and from the bathroom when they went to shower. The family norm was not to wear clothes at these times. Everyone was fine with this until one day the nine-year-old daughter started wearing a robe when she went to shower. The father was telling this story with sadness, having concluded that she had somehow learned to be ashamed of her body and to feel negatively towards it. I suggested an alternative interpretation of his daughter's behavior: she had reached the age where she wanted to assert her choice about her body space. She was defining her need for privacy which was a healthy boundary for her. The father was surprised but thoughtful at my interpretation. He fortunately had not punished her or made fun of her choice. He had allowed her to make her choice and thereby challenge the family norm. But now he could also see that it was a positive sign in her development and he could affirm her choice in a new way.

Even in an intimate, sexual relationship, boundaries are important. Intimacy does not mean the absence of boundaries. Intimacy means that boundaries are more fluid and permeable because there is trust between two people. And those boundaries continue to be negotiated and renegotiated throughout a relationship. For example, in the early days of their relationship, Vanessa noticed that Jerome would stop and squeeze her breasts whenever he walked by her in their home. At first Vanessa was flattered and enjoyed his affection. But after a while, she began to be aggravated by this repeated touch. So she talked to him about it. She told him that she didn't like it that he seemed to presume that he could touch her breasts whenever he wanted to. She said that sometimes it felt good and she liked it, and other times it didn't. She asked him how he would feel if every time she walked past him she would grab his crotch. He winced and seemed to understand. He didn't get defensive; he apologized. But he wasn't sure what to do differently. He asked her how he would know which was which. She said, "You'll just have to ask." Touch boundaries in an intimate relationship can never be taken for granted.

For those of us who, by accident of birth or virtue of acquired status, possess power and resources vis-à-vis another person, there is a particular responsibility to use our power and resources justly and to carefully guard the boundaries of the helping relationship. Whether as parent, teacher, minister, therapist, or doctor, we are in a position where we can easily take advantage of the vulnerability of the other person.

If a client trusts her therapist to know what is best for her, and if that therapist tells her that in order to deal with her marital problems, she should have sex with him, she is likely to submit willingly to his suggestion. She respects his power and authority as her therapist, which then may undercut her own best judgment. This ploy is even more effective when utilized by a clergyperson who carries the additional authority of moral and spiritual guide. If a minister tells a congregant that God has brought them together, that their "love" could never be wrong, that to know God truly, the congregant should explore sexual intimacy with the minister, the congregant's sense of morality is compromised. Her/his moral guide is adroitly explaining and encouraging sexual activity with her/him. The power and authority of the minister often supersedes the best judgment of the congregant. Her/his moral agency may be undercut by the minister's misuse of his power in her/his life.

When we find ourselves on the less powerful side of a relationship—anytime we are a client, for example—we need to be realistic about boundaries. Having sex with a therapist, minister, doctor, teacher, or any helping professional is not going to solve any of our problems, but it will definitely create new ones. We may feel sexually attracted to someone to whom we go for professional help. This is not unusual and it can be confusing.* It is relatively easy for an unethical professional to take advantage of our feelings and confusion. But do not be deceived. Sexual advances from someone whom we have sought out for help in a professional relationship has nothing to do with serving our best interests. In order to gain the benefits supposedly inherent in a helping relationship, sexual boundaries must be maintained. Parents, teacher, ministers, therapists, etc. are not our peers when we seek them out professionally (see chapter 5, "Choosing Peer Relationships"). When we are in a non-peer relationship with them, we are particularly vulnerable to exploitation and abuse if they are not clear on their responsibility to maintain boundaries even if we push those boundaries.

To exercise one's moral choice to say "no" to the sexual advances of one's therapist, minister, or teacher who does not want to hear "no," will in all likelihood result in negative consequences such as loss of the relationship, ridicule, or poor grades or recommendations. These consequences signal a coercive relationship in which we were not supposed to have the option to say "no." The same dynamic can occur in a sexual relationship with someone

---

* In our culture, many women find power sexually attractive and many men find powerlessness sexually attractive. The dominant/submissive model of relationship has become eroticized. This makes the male therapist or pastor relating to the female client or congregant especially risky. See Peter Rutter, *Sex in the Forbidden Zone* (Los Angeles: J.P. Tarcher, 1989), for further discussion.

you thought was a peer. Here a partner may use emotional black-mail to try to talk you into sexual activity and if you say "no," may withdraw from the relationship, ridicule you for being "uptight," or use physical force or violence to accomplish intercourse or other sexual contact. This punishing behavior is the surest indicator that this relationship was not one of mutual respect and authentic consent (see chapter 6, "Authentic Consent").

Common Sense

Respect for boundaries is not the same as rigidity of boundaries. Only when we respect boundaries and can see the risks involved in crossing them can we make careful, informed choices about their flexibility. Professional boundaries can be flexible but they should not be fluid. If we understand power and vulnerability in relationships, then we can understand the importance of boundaries to help us avoid either misusing our power or being taken advantage of. Once we acknowledge the reality of power and vulnerability, common sense can carry us a long way. If we truly respect the other person, whether they are our employee, client, or partner, and if we stay aware of our own needs and feelings, then we will be motivated to respect their boundaries and act accordingly. Our behaviors may even become second nature.

We will make plenty of mistakes and cross plenty of boundaries in our relationships with others. The point is not to be without fault, but rather to understand that how we deal with those mistakes is what matters. When Vanessa confronted Jerome about not wanting him to constantly touch her breasts, he could have become defensive and insistent upon his right to touch her whenever and wherever he wanted. He could have done that and lived with the consequences, which would be the loss of her trust of him and a diminishment of their intimacy. But he wisely chose to listen and respect her wishes, which was a sign to her that he could be trusted and that the intimacy of their relationship could grow even deeper. After all, isn't this the point?

4 The Particularities of Heterosexuality

> The Bible contains six admonishments to homosexuals and 362 admonishments to heterosexuals. That doesn't mean that God doesn't love heterosexuals. It's just that they need more supervision.
>
> —Comedian Lynn Lavner

✂ MOST OF YOU WHO READ THIS BOOK are heterosexuals, that is, your primary sexual and emotional preference is a person of the opposite sex. Relating to someone of the opposite sex is the numerically and psychologically dominant mode of intimate relationships in late twentieth-century western culture.* Virtually all means of communicating social norms and constructing social reality provide explicit and implicit directions on how to behave in a heterosexual relationship. Movies, advertising, popular music, romance novels, pornography, religious teachings, Bible stories, peer information, soap operas, and the like provide extensive training on how to look, how to act, and what to buy in order to be a successful heterosexual. Heterosexuality does not require any organized effort to carry out this agenda. It is self-perpetuating and provides its own mechanisms to shape and control behavior. It is normative and determines what is normative.

---

* Indeed, Adrienne Rich suggests that it is compulsory (Rich, 1980). This means that because of prejudice and homophobia, many people feel that they have no choice but to live a heterosexual lifestyle regardless of their sexual orientation.

Heterosexuality in all its manifestations takes place within a patriarchal context where, by virtue of gender, there is a difference in power between men and women. Thus heterosexual relationships present particular dilemmas for women and men of conscience.* How is it possible to be in a heterosexual relationship with integrity in a culture in which men are expected to be dominant and women are expected to be submissive, in which the control of women by men is the foundation for heterosexuality? Listen to any AM radio station for thirty minutes, read any newspaper, watch virtually any film, or any soap opera on any day of the week, pick up any piece of pornography, read virtually any book on the *New York Times* best seller list, and you will see and hear the predominant themes of heterosexuality as we know it. Men are portrayed as brutal, controlling, and arrogant, and women as either helpless victims or as manipulative, deceptive, promiscuous beings who, because of their behavior, deserve what men do to them—making the circle complete.

The real kicker is that this particular power relationship is then promoted and experienced as erotic. Remember the classic scene in *Gone With the Wind?* Rhett Butler and Scarlett O'Hara are arguing; he tries to kiss her; she resists; he picks her up and carries her up the grand staircase. The film cuts to Scarlett waking up alone in bed the next morning, smiling, radiant, and happy. Although this movie was produced before sexual scenes were explicit, the dramatic implication is clear: Butler took O'Hara to her bed in spite of her resistance and forced her to have sexual intercourse. The next morning, she is delighted by the whole affair. This is the romantic picture repeated over and over, only now in films the sex scene is explicit and usually more violent. Men and women find themselves in a dominant/submissive scenario in which dominance is eroticized for men and submission is eroticized for women. In other words, the male's dominance and

---

* This phrase is used by John Stoltenberg to describe men who do not accept the patriarchal norms of relationships and who actively confront sexism.

control is portrayed in the media as sexy and corresponds to the female's submission or powerlessness which is also portrayed as sexy. Real men are in control of *their* women; real women long to be possessed by *their* men.

Sexology, the supposed scientific study of sexuality, has been a major contributor for decades to the normalization of the dominant/ submissive norm for heterosexuality. In *Ideal Marriage*, the virtual Bible of sexology from 1930–1965, the Dutch sexologist Van de Velde wrote:

> What both man and woman, driven by *obscure primitive urges* [italics mine], wish to feel in the sexual act, is the essential force of *maleness*, which expresses itself in a sort of violent and absolute *possession* of the woman. And so both of them can and do exult in a certain degree of male aggression and dominance—whether actual or apparent—which proclaims this essential force.[1]

The same message was updated in 1969 in *The Intimate Enemy—How to Fight Fair in Love and Marriage*, which was still in print in 1994:

> Women, especially during the uncertainties of seduction and early courtship, will accommodate to the male level of aggression assigned to them. They usually keep secret their own desire for more or less tenderness. . . . As partners learn how to fuse sex and aggression, their sex satisfaction gradually increases and their need to injure others verbally or physically decreases.[2]

Don't assume that such notions are outdated. Alex Comfort in *The New Joy of Sex: The Gourmet Guide to Lovemaking for the Nineties* continues in the same vein: "If you haven't learned that sexual violence can be tender and tenderness violent, you haven't begun to play as real lovers. . . . To need some degree of violence in sex . . . is statistically pretty normal."[3] At least one clinical professional, Bernie Zilbergeld, offered a critique of this message in 1978:

With all the grinding and slamming and banging portrayed in the media, and with the absence of good examples of more tender lovemaking, it is not surprising that many men think of sex as a rough and tough business and that they will be most appreciated if they pummel the hell out of their partner. Since women in fantasyland are always grateful to the most aggressive and even violent lovers, [à la Rhett and Scarlett, *et al*] and since there is a clear implication that a man who cannot brutalize a woman is something less than a man, there is considerable pressure for a man to restrain his more tender expression of affection and give free rein to his more aggressive tendencies.[4]

John Stoltenberg more recently questioned the norms of male sexuality in our culture:

So why is it that some of us with penises think it's sexy to pressure someone into having sex against their will? Some of us actually get harder the harder the person resists. Some of us with penises actually believe that some of us without penises want to be raped. And why is it that some of us with penises think it's sexy to treat other people as objects, as things to be bought and sold, impersonal bodies to be possessed and consumed for our sexual pleasure? Why is it that some of us with penises are aroused by sex tinged with rape, and sex commoditized by pornography? Why do so many of us with penises want such antisexual sex?[5]

Why indeed? Unfortunately, heterosexual men have learned their script very well.

Heterosexual women's version of this script is repeatedly portrayed in the media, especially in romance novels in which the heroine longs to be possessed, taken, or violated in some way. Women, too, have learned their script all too well. The extreme of this garden variety dominant/submissive scenario is sadomasochism. Here the dominant/submissive role-playing becomes the centerpiece of the individuals' erotic experience. The power play itself is the primary source of sexual arousal.*

Is it possible for heterosexual women and men who are distressed and alienated by this merry-go-round to somehow disembark? Is it possible to be in a healthy heterosexual relationship in which there is mutual respect, equality, justice, *and* sexual satisfaction in spite of all of the messages to the contrary? Yes, because not everyone accepts the dominant/submissive scenario which is presented as heterosexual romance. But not to participate in this milieu requires an acute awareness on the part of both men and women of the powerful social forces and expectations which seek to define us all, and a conscious commitment to swim against the tide. If we are to swim against it and avoid drowning, we must first learn to recognize it.

How Are Women and Men Socialized to Relate?

In our culture, despite major demographic and sociological shifts in the family, the political arena and the workplace, and despite over two decades of public debate about women's role in both private and public spheres, women are still generally taught to be dependent on men and to live their lives primarily in an effort to please men, believing that, in some way, their self-interest is served by these efforts. Women are encouraged to be attracted to men's power—which is not altogether irrational in this scenario. Some women see in men's power the possibility of protection from what they perceive as an unsafe world; that is, from other men's violence. Of course the price they are likely to pay for this protection is very high indeed.

---

* There is nothing exclusively heterosexual about s/m. Some gays and lesbians also participate in dominant/submissive sexual activities. But what is revealing about the influence of the heterosexual norm is that even in a same-sex s/m encounter, the dominant/submissive role-playing often correlates with male/female role-playing. See Sheila Jeffreys, *The Lesbian Heresy* (London: The Women's Press, 1994).

Men continue to be taught that it is a man's world, that they have access (depending on their race and class) to resources, that women's job is to take care of them, and that they can have what they want when they want it and use physical force if necessary to get it. The point of intersection for women and men is violence: women are taught to fear men's violence, to expect men's violence—especially in the family—and men are taught that they have the option to use violence—especially in the family.

Our training as women and men begins very early. Psychologist Ellyn Kaschak observes:

> [Boys] will be taught that a certain amount of threat to women is an acceptable expression of masculinity. In normal [sic] development, young boys begin to express sexual interest in girls by mild forms of teasing, as each era finds appropriate: dunking girls' pigtails in the inkwell, producing bugs, snakes, or other animals of which girls are supposed to be fearful, et cetera. These are well-condensed statements of the traditional heterosexual contract and the template for later adult relationships. She is supposed to be fearful and vulnerable. He frightens as well as protects her. Her vulnerability and his power to frighten and to protect supposedly enhance his masculinity and sexuality, as well as her femininity and sexual interest.[6]

The "games" of heterosexual interaction establish not only a behavioral norm but a context of dominance and submission as an erotically charged expectation for adult men and women.

I once observed a five-year-old girl and boy playing in the school yard. The boy hit the girl hard and she ran to her mother nearby, seeking sympathy for her pain. Her mother chastised her for being upset and explained that the boy hitting her meant that he liked her. This experience echoed loudly in my brain reminding me of a fifteen-year-old girl who, after my two-hour discussion of dating violence with her church youth group announced, "Well, all I know is that I don't think my boyfriend really loves me. He hasn't hit me yet." In that moment I knew that in trying to address dating violence among teenagers, I was swimming not just against the tide, but against a tidal wave.

"Heterosexual Courtship Violence"

The heterosexual pattern of relating is usually established early in relationships in what researchers call "heterosexual courtship violence." This term names the dominant/submissive dynamic which is encouraged in the early stages of heterosexual relationships where the violence may be subtle or overt but the goal is control of the woman. These patterns are particularly clear in adolescent experiences which provide the early training for adult relationships. Larkin and Popaleni's research on adolescent dating is revealing:

> The pre-adolescent girl escapes much . . . demeaning behavior because she spends most of her time with other females. . . . However, as she enters adolescence the young female is more vulnerable to abuse by males for three reasons. First because women are taught that their value is determined by their ability to attract men, most heterosexual young women will perceive themselves as "Lacking at the very core when not in a relationship with a man" (Seigel, 1988:117) and so they may opt to spend more time in mixed-sex settings. Second, boys as they grow older recognize their privileged position and realize that this position can only be maintained by force. Third, young women's sexual development becomes visible and young men begin to see them primarily as sexual beings. . . .[7]

The impact of these three factors on young women is profound. Consider the experience of a college student who tried to communicate and negotiate in an intimate relationship in which she initially assumed that she had some power:

> We talked about what we expected from each other before. We were to date each other exclusively. We talked about having sex but decided not to because I was not ready. It seemed pretty

much agreed upon that it would be that way. We started to talk about marriage, again the subject of sex came up. He felt that it would be all right since we were practically engaged. I didn't feel that way but I felt I was not being fair to him. I got to the point where I didn't know what to do. I felt that I should do it for him but inside I knew I would regret it. We talked many times about this. I started to dread seeing him because he would always bring it up. He'd say it was right because we loved each other, or if you loved me you would want me as much as I want you. I began to question my feelings for him and my decision not to go to bed with him. I went for help. I needed someone to talk to so I went to the Health Center. They helped me work through my feelings and reconfirmed my right to the way I felt. We talked one night about why I felt the way I did and I felt he understood. He seemed content with our decision. We went on as we were and the subject didn't come up. One night we went out. It was very pleasant and I knew we would be all right then—but I was dead wrong. He had too much to drink and when we got back he decided he would do what he wanted. It all happened so fast. Afterwards I felt guilty. I couldn't believe it! I felt used and degraded. I got to the point that I hated him for what he had done to me. I tried to rationalize things by saying his love for me got out of control but I realized love had nothing to do with what had happened. After a lot of therapy I realized that it really wasn't my fault and that I can't let it ruin my self-respect. I will continue to hold on to my values about what my future relationships will entail even after that. It hurts but I will survive.[8]

Some of you have had this experience, and most of you, female or male, have not called it rape. Clearly there was an abundance of communication between these two people but to no avail. The bottom line was that "he decided he would do what he wanted" against the will of his partner.

Heterosexual courtship violence takes many forms, but its primary goal is to teach women to submit to men and to attend to male needs: in other words, to establish and reinforce male power over women. The question of women's needs or desires is never an issue. A woman's submissive behavior may not even be conscious on her part; a man's individual dominant behavior may also not be conscious. But both take place in a context which promotes and reinforces this interaction between them as normative.

In listening to the stories of teenage girls, researchers suggest three categories for the behaviors of heterosexual courtship violence: diminishment, intimidation, and force. They cite acts of diminishment which objectify and degrade young women. The male behavior includes criticism, rating, and the display of pornographic material.[9] For example, in school, boys use a numerical system to rate a girl's attractiveness; they will stand in the hall and hold up rating cards numbered 1–10 as girls walk past. When one girl objected to this practice, she received a zero rating. In addition to sexual diminishment, many young women of color also are subject to racism: white girls are rated higher than African-American girls.[10]

Acts of intimidation include threats and surveillance used to warn young women of the violent consequences when they challenge their assigned position.[11] For example, one young man poured his beer on a young woman at his table. She responded by threatening to pour her drink on him. He warned her, "Do that, and I'll rape you." Jealousy motivates surveillance of young women. One young woman described a situation in which she would baby-sit for a friend, a woman she really liked and respected. "'[My boyfriend] would telephone seventeen times while I was babysitting. He would look in the windows when I was there with the kids because he thought I was having an affair with [the woman]. He just thought I was having affairs with everyone. He was possessive . . . more than I can even describe.'"[12]

Acts of force are used to punish young women who choose to resist their designated subordinate position.[13] For example, one young woman described her experience: "'He didn't hit me, but he would twist my arms or other mean things. Or he'd pinch me really hard when we were around other people. Then I would yell at him and he would say, "What's your problem?" He'd act as if he'd done nothing. And then, I'd look like a fool.'"[14] The threat of physical danger is also used by young men to gain a date's compliance to have sex. The practice of isolating young women in cars, after dark, and in remote settings can be very intimidating. One young woman who was on a date with a new boyfriend had decided she did not want to have sex with him. But she was afraid he would leave her stranded at midnight, miles from home and any assistance unless she complied with his demand for sex.[15]

What are the Consequences—For Women?

Both women and men pay a high price for trying to fit into heterosexuality as it is promoted in our culture. Fundamentally, both miss an opportunity for authentic relationship, a chance to know another person and be known by another person in an intimate relationship. But women pay the higher price.

Larkin and Popaleni summarize the impact of heterosexual courtship violence on young women:

> Boyfriends' acts of diminishment, intimidation and force operate to limit young women's personal development. For example, boyfriends' surveillance of their girlfriends' socializing with other young women, and subsequent accusations of lesbianism, resulted in many young women terminating friendships with other young women which had offered them enjoyment and support in times of crisis. Moreover, boyfriends' abusive behaviour eroded young women's psychological and emotional abilities to determine for themselves their own terms and boundaries for self-development. Enmeshed in relationships which encourage self-doubt and self-reproach, some young women put a definitive end to their involvement in such self-development activities as team sports, musical presentations and drama clubs. . . . The restrictions imposed on young women through the perpetual threat of male violence have the attendant consequence of limiting

their power and control in the larger world, because so much of their behaviour is geared to securing their own safety. It is precisely this required pre-occupation with ensuring their own physical and psychological survival that precludes young women from focusing on the most important aspect of their personal development: themselves.[16]

Young women's loss of self and the expenditure of enormous energy on psychic and physical survival are perhaps the most tragic and profound price of the dominant/submissive arrangement of contemporary heterosexuality. One adolescent girl summed up her feelings: "I almost feel like I lost my old self, like she's not here anymore . . . and I kind of miss her, sometimes. She was a fun person. I loved her."[17] The inevitable loss of self which is recognized very early by many women is manifested, for example, in the loss of her name and the taking of a husband's name in marriage. Just as the name change announces a change in her identity (she is known now for her relationship with a man rather than for herself) so the context of heterosexual expectations dramatically diminishes who she is and what she believes to be her real options in the world.

For adult women, the consequences continue. Sandra Lee Bartky makes this observation:

> The woman who checks her makeup half a dozen times a day to see if her foundation has caked or her mascara has run, who worries that the wind or the rain may spoil her hairdo, who looks frequently to see if her stockings have bagged at the ankle or who, feeling fat, monitors everything she eats, has become . . . a self committed to a relentless self-surveillance. This self-surveillance is a form of obedience to patriarchy. It is also the reflection in the woman's consciousness of the fact that *she* is under surveillance in ways that *he* is not, that whatever else she may become, she is importantly a body designed to please or excite. The script is clearly presented day in and day out and relentlessly taught at every stage of her development. For her it is normative

to be concerned consciously or unconsciously about what men think because her job is to serve the needs of men."[18]

There are several motivations for a heterosexual woman's self-surveillance. She wants to be noticed by men, desired by men, accepted by men, protected by men: all of these can be achieved if she plays her role well. If she chooses otherwise and does not dress, act, or speak in the ways which men accept, she knows that she puts herself at risk. She will likely be punished for stepping out of role. Not only her sense of self-worth but also her physical safety may be dependent on her acting ability.

Based on experiences of abuse or stories about other girls' or women's experiences of abuse, all women learn that the world is not a safe place, and this just because we are female. Women have to cope with the ever-present threat of male violence regardless of age, race, class, sexual orientation, or physical ability. Women's ways of coping usually mean adjusting behaviors to accommodate the external reality of male violence. "Women know instinctively where and how to walk in public in order to avoid danger as much as possible. . . . Most women learn how to behave in private situations, learn that relationships give them safety and security— and many keep believing this even when it isn't so."[19] Women monitor their behavior constantly in public and in private, hoping, praying, believing, that they can avoid male displeasure, anger, and violence.

—For Men?

Many men accept the prerogatives and privileges which come to them in patriarchy by virtue of their gender. Many heterosexual men expect women to meet their needs emotionally, sexually, and physically. In order to ensure that their intimate partner carries out these functions, men are allowed to employ a variety of methods to control her behavior. These methods range from subtle coercion to the threat of or use of physical violence. What is the down side of this for a man? The biggest negative consequence is that he never has a real relationship with his partner. He is not trustworthy, he is not real; he is lonely and isolated. He may have a person who cooks for him, cleans up after him, takes orders from him, and serves as a sexual aid. He may be fulfilling a role he has learned from watching John Wayne, Clint Eastwood, Arnold Schwartzenegger, Bruce Willis, or MTV or listening to 2 Live Crew or Snoop Doggy Dog. He may be turned on by the knowledge that his partner is dependent on him or afraid of him. He may be trying to live up to the expectations of his male peers who believe that real men score, know how to control "their" women, and are always in charge.

For a man to choose not to play this game is certain to result in ridicule, ostracism, or violence from other men. As I stood in the check-out line one day, the clerk and the customer behind me were engaged in a conversation about their children. The customer asked, "How is your son Jason? He's a senior, isn't he? Is he playing football this year?" The other mother replied, "Yes. He doesn't want to but he is." The customer queried, "If he doesn't want to, why is he playing?" "Because he doesn't want them to make fun of him, think he's a pansy." Such a man is not a real man; such a man must be "queer." There are consequences for stepping out of role for men as well as women.

Homophobia, the fear of homosexuality or of gay and lesbian people, is the big stick which is used to keep both men and women playing their parts in this drama. Real women don't have friendships with other women and hence are cut off from the support and reality check they need. Real men play sports, join the military or the gang whether they want to or not. Real men don't have friendships with women either—real men have sex with women, not friendship.

The Dilemma

The dilemma for the heterosexual woman is particularly acute. Your male partner (or partner to be) is a product of, and has chosen to either accept or struggle against, the patriarchal norms which grant him power and privilege, including the option to use force to control you. How can you trust him? How can you let yourself be open to him? How can you develop a peer relationship with him? The answer, in short: against all odds and with a great deal of effort.

For the heterosexual man of conscience, there is also a dilemma. How can you give up these privileges and prerogatives? Why should you? If you believe that the way things are is not the way they have to be, that you are missing out on something, that you do not want to be dominant in an intimate relationship, then you have a real choice to make in this matter. If you exercise this choice, you may discover some of the same things about relating sexually that Stoltenberg discovered:

> Like others born with a penis, I was born into a sex-class system that requires my collaboration every day, even in how I have sex. Nobody told me, when I was younger, that I could have noncoital sex and that it would be fine. Actually, much better than fine. Nobody told me about an incredible range of other erotic possibilities for mutual lovemaking—multiple, nonejaculatory orgasms; including the feeling you get when even the tiniest place where you and your partner touch becomes like a window through which great tidal storms of passion ebb and flow, back and forth. Nobody told me about the sex you can have when you stop working at having a sex. My body told me, finally. And I began to trust what my body was telling me more than the lie I was supposed to make real.[20]

So What Is to be Done?

It is a paradox that during the so-called sexual revolution of the last twenty-five years, women won the right to say "yes" to sexual activity and have all but lost the right to say "no." The disclosure and wide public discussion of the frequency of date rape among undergraduates* has resulted in some colleges and universities initiating prevention efforts. In addition to education and consciousness raising, some have instituted policies. At Antioch College in Ohio, the policy *written by students* says, "Verbal consent should be obtained with each new level of physical and/or sexual contact/conduct in any given interaction regardless of who initiates it." These efforts are attempts to help students think and communicate with each other about some very important matters. Conversation has certainly ensued.

In her book, *The Morning After*, Katie Roiphe states: "There is a gray area in which someone's rape may be another person's bad night."

Syndicated columnist Ellen Goodman responded: "In a book that ripples with uncertainty beneath the crisp veneer of her argument, she says that the current campus obsession with sexual assault and sexual codes of ethics are part of a sexual counterrevolution."

Roiphe also states: "'The assumption embedded in the movement against date rape is our grandmother's assumption [that] 'Men want sex, women don't.' There is a return to stereotypes of 'boys as a sexual threat, girls as vulnerable . . . men as hunters, women as hunted.'"

---

* The MS. survey of 6,100 undergraduates found "One in four female respondents had had an experience that met the legal definition of rape or attempted rape." (p. 2) "Nearly all (95 percent) involved only one rapist. Most of the women (84 percent) knew the men who attacked them, with more than half the assaults happening on dates. . . . The average amount of force used by the men was rated as moderate, usually twisting the victim's arm or holding her down. Only 9 percent of the women said their rapists hit them; 5 percent were threatened with weapons. Most (84 percent) tried unsuccessfully to reason with the men and many (70 percent) put up some form of physical resistance." (p. 49) Robin Warshaw, *I Never Called It Rape* (New York: MS. Foundation for Education and Communication, Inc. and Sarah Lazin Books, 1988).

Goodman counters: "I don't think that the new sexual codes of conduct signal some retreat to Puritanism . . . . I think that they are, rather, part of an ongoing struggle to create a new single standard."[21]

Actually, our mothers and grandmothers were probably more right than we'd like to acknowledge. It wasn't that they were anti-sex; it was that they knew all too well that boys and men who subscribe to the dominant heterosexual norms are dangerous to girls and women. They knew from experience and they wanted to do what they could to insure that we did not have those same experiences.

Policies on campuses seem to have created a firestorm of reaction which indicates that we've hit the nail on the head. The analysis behind the Antioch policies goes to the source of the problem and argues for a balancing of power in a peer relationship in which both partners take responsibility for their sexual interaction. Most who argue against this approach are concerned that it takes all the fun out of sex; fun being the male's prerogative to use coercion and force to get what he wants.

Of course rules, standards, and policies are only a means to an end. Robert Hahn states the task for heterosexual men:

> The challenge is not to gain a woman's consent for each touching or sexual gesture, but to create and maintain an environment in which consent or denial are not threatened by violence. It is only in such a setting that consent becomes meaningful. . . . Thus, for a man to establish a relationship with a woman in which consent is a possibility, he must make the context of interaction a domination-free, voluntary zone.[22]

For men, this requires that you renounce your option to use force or the threat of force to get your own way. It requires that you give up being in control in your intimate relationship. Against all odds, against all norms and roles you have learned, in spite of most of your peers, you, as a moral agent, can choose to forego coercion, control, and force, and relate to your partner with respect and as an equal. This option rests on the assumption that it is more important to you to be in a real intimate relationship with another human being than to be in charge or than to be popular with your male peers.

The task for heterosexual women is to expect more from men, to refuse anything less than a just relationship, to use the resources of self-esteem, information and peer support and, if necessary, the legal system to sustain you in choosing something different than the scripts you have been offered. This requires that you be willing to see that your interests are not well-served by dependency on men or by subsuming your identity beneath a man's, that you have a right to respect, safety, and support in relationship with a man, and that you are a whole person whether or not you are in such a relationship. You also have the capacity as a moral agent to make your choices based on this awareness and a responsibility to say "no" to a relationship which lacks the respect you deserve.

If a heterosexual relationship is going to work, women need to expect more and men need to expect less. Don't expect her to meet all your needs, to anticipate your needs, to take care of all your maintenance needs (clothing, food, doctors' appointments, etc.), to be available for sex whenever you want it, to totally accommodate her life to yours, to have no independent thoughts and ideas of her own, to agree with all of your opinions including your politics and religion, to take care of the children alone, to, when you say "jump", ask "how high?"

Expect him to listen to you, to respect your opinions and ideas, to keep his promises, to share responsibility for safe sex and contraception, to share parenting of children, to share maintenance of your home, to pick up his own dry-cleaning, to respect your privacy and private time, to respect your friends outside of the relationship, to understand that "no" means no and "yes" means yes, to treat you as a peer, and never to use force to get his way even if he is twice as big as you are.

There is an indigenous group of people in the Philippines who do not understand the concept of a man forcing a woman to have sex. "Why would anyone do that?" they ask. "Sex is something you do with someone you like." What a concept! For those of you who make this choice, there is a possibility of salvaging real relationships from our patriarchal heritage which continues to deny equality, justice, intimacy, trust, and pleasure between lovers.

PART II
Guidelines for Relationships

5 Choosing Peer Relationships

... it is you, my equal, my companion, my familiar friend with whom I kept pleasant company ...

—Psalm 55:13–14 NRSV

There is one kind of marriage that has not been tried and that is a contract made by equal parties to lead an equal life, with equal restraints and privileges on either side.

—Elizabeth Cady Stanton

Guideline #1. Is my choice of intimate partner a peer, i.e. someone whose power is relatively equal to mine? We must limit our sexual interaction to our peers. Some people are off limits for our sexual interests.

✀ IF ONE WERE TO LOOK to the mainstream media for information about the norm of sexual relationships, one would find the following generalizations:

1. Sexual relationships are heterosexual.
2. There is a single standard of beauty and attractiveness for all women that ignores differences of age, race, or size.
3. Women are attracted to men who are powerful, strong, wealthy, of high social or professional status, from their own racial/ethnic group, and who are older and taller than they are.

4. Men are attracted to women who are powerless, weak, silent, stereotypically beautiful, with no professional status, from their own racial/ethnic group, and who are physically smaller and younger than they are.

These are the norms of who women and men are and what relationships are whether the source is MTV, soft- or hard-core pornography, evangelical broadcasting, advertising, soap operas, movies, music, or romance novels. There are virtually no norms portrayed of women or men in same-sex relationships, of women and men in a relationship between equals, or of two people in an interracial relationship. The implication is that these relationships don't exist.

These expectations are a reflection of the socially constructed male-dominated sociopolitical context in which we all live, that is, patriarchy. This may sound like ideological rhetoric but it isn't. It is a description of the way things are in contemporary western culture. Patriarchy describes a social order in which men as a class have more power and resources than women as a class, and in which the status quo of gender inequality is reinforced by custom, attitude, and practice. Unfortunately, this inequality is accepted and reinforced by the majority of people. The most dominant feature of this status quo is the presumption that men have power over women or that someone has power over someone else. The norms remain consistent even when the variables of race, class, and age are added.

As a result, the image of dominant/submissive relationships has become eroticized. In sexual relationships, someone is bigger and stronger than the other, someone is on top while someone else is on the bottom, someone is in charge while the other follows along. This phenomenon is abundantly clear in pornography where the source of the heterosexual male viewer's sexual arousal appears to be not merely the sexual explicitness of the images but the subjugation and humiliation of women. In child pornography, this reality is even more clearly drawn. The absolute powerlessness and vulnerability of a child who is totally under the control of the adult is one source of the adult's sexual arousal. The dominant/submissive theme is frequently used in gay and lesbian pornography as well.

The predominant erotic socialization for heterosexual men and women in our late twentieth-century culture is the powerful, controlling male sexually serviced by the compliant, submissive female or child. In this scenario, the self-centered male gets what he wants, when he wants it, with no regard for his partner's wishes and no responsibility for her well-being. He is completely unencumbered; he takes what he regards as rightfully his. The woman or child willingly submits, it seems.

Do not quickly dismiss this depressing situation as merely the figment of the media's imagination. If we place this picture side by side with the reality described by most victims of sexual and domestic violence, we see a painful consistency. The reported cases of rape, child sexual abuse, incest, sexual harassment, and marital rape are only the most extreme manifestations of this pattern of dominance/submission. Men who travel to Asia seeking sex with Asian women, or who "order" an Asian bride through the mail, are very forthright in their reasoning: back home women are too uppity, they say. They want a docile woman who knows how to take orders and not talk back. In depicting powerful men and powerless women, the media are reflecting reality as well as perpetuating and justifying it.

When gender is not an issue, that is, in same-sex intimate relationships, there are some gays and lesbians who have adopted the heterosexual norm of dominance and submission. Those who ascribe to this norm seem to parrot the heterosexual notion that inequality is essential to sexual arousal. They have incorporated masculine/feminine role-playing into their relationships and sexual activity in order to participate in the dominant/submissive model. It is a sad commentary on the power of the dominant/submissive norm that even some of those who reject heterosexuality are nonetheless bound by the norms which it promotes.

Why would anyone want to submit to this arrangement in which they are humiliated, controlled, abused, and exploited? How could they possibly see this as in their best interests? In order to understand this phenomenon, it is necessary to understand how childhood abuse can affect its victims:

> In the mind of the beaten child, violence as an exercise of control equals love. In the mind of the raped daughter, sex as an exercise of power equals love. . . . Love, sex, and violence are intertwined in our minds. . . We take that construction with us into our adult lives to enact and re-enact in intimate contexts.[1]

Sadomasochism, the extreme practice of eroticized dominance/submission, is often linked to childhood abuse:

> Practitioners defend S/M by stating that it is the only way they can experience sexual pleasure because their abuse has tied abuse and pleasure so closely together for them that any possibility of an eroticism of equality is locked out.[2]

While many survivors of childhood abuse find healing and support and are able to reject that childhood linkage of abuse/arousal choosing instead to seek another way, others do not. Sheila Jeffreys, in *Lesbian Heresy*, makes this observation and critique:

> It is helpful to an understanding of sadomasochism to see it as a form of self-injury. This self-injury can be purely emotional or physical. . . . Self-injurers feel a compulsive urge towards cutting, of wrists, throat or other parts of the body, injury with lighted cigarettes, attempts at suicide. The compulsion can be kept at bay for months at a time but then tends to return. In S/M practice another person performs the injury but at the behest of the self-mutilator. . . . While most people would consider self-injury in non-sexual forms to be undesirable and would find it unacceptable that panel discussions should take place as to whether

such self-injury was positive or negative, sadomasochism is seen as being about sex and therefore beyond serious criticism.[3]

This uncritical acceptance is one of the most disturbing aspects of the promotion of sadomasochism in sexual relationships. Just because a particular behavior is arousing does not make it good, appropriate, or acceptable. We have choices about how we shape our own eroticism in adulthood, even if we have a history of abuse. If we are committed to do least harm to self and other, we will reject an eroticism that is based on dominance and submission.

In our society, inequality based on dominance/submission is eroticized for both men and women. The possibility of relating intimately to a peer, one who has relatively equal power and as a result will require conversation, negotiation, and compromise in relationship, is generally not encouraged, supported, or modeled. Those of us who seek out such a relationship, whether heterosexual, lesbian, gay, or bisexual, find ourselves with virtually a blank slate which can be both blessing and curse.*

The Eroticization of Equality

What would happen if equality itself was an erotic experience? The possibility of a relationship with someone who is equally strong, capable, self-confident, and clear about her/his interests and desires seems most attractive if one is really interested in a relationship: that is, in spending time with someone in an experience of intimacy and trust. Such a relationship requires time, energy, conversation, and compromise. But the payoff is well worth the investment. Equality can be very erotic.

---

* The current backlash against feminism and the cynicism of postmodernism argue that intimate relationship between equals are impossible, undesirable, and generally old-fashioned. Jeffreys counters: "Being a feminist meant, and still means to many, being a conscientious objector who willfully and rebelliously refuses to enter the games of gender and dominance and submission, and believes, despite postmodernist scepticism, that it is possible to live outside them." (*The Lesbian Heresy*, p. 138)

For example, I like to play pitch and catch. I prefer to play with someone who is of similar size and strength to me or who is willing not to use greater size and strength to overwhelm me. I like to both pitch and catch, and I assume that she does as well. I like variety in both. Sometimes I like to throw a high, pop fly. Sometimes I like to catch a grounder. But if she doesn't like to catch pop flies then I won't throw them. We both wear protective equipment otherwise known as gloves. I wear a baseball cap to keep the sun out of my eyes and to look cute. We talk about a variety of things while we play. I try not to throw at her face because that is dangerous and no fun for her. She tries not to throw pitches that she knows I can't catch. When either of us gets tired, we stop. The pleasure in playing pitch and catch is twofold: we are sharing a playful physical activity that we both enjoy, and for me, to make a really good pitch or a solid catch feels terrific. Sort of like sex.

What could be more exciting and satisfying than being with a partner who freely *chooses* to be with you, who, given the option of other people or activities which he/she could have chosen, instead has chosen you? She/he is not with you out of fear or obligation but because she/he *wants* to be. He/she listens and respects your opinions and desires. You and she/he are both there to give and receive sexually and emotionally. You are there to have fun together and enjoy each other.

Likewise she/he is not there to serve you, to meet all of your needs at the expense of her/his own, to say "no" when she/he means "yes," to pretend she/he doesn't have an opinion or a skill different from yours. He/she is not there to always take the initiative, have all the answers, or make all the decisions.

Why have so many women learned that the only sexual scenario that is arousing is one in which her partner overcomes her resistance, in which she is "taken"? What is romantic about this? Why have so many men learned that they must always be in charge and in control? Perhaps it provides the illusion that everyone is actually relieved of taking responsibility for their individual needs and desires.

Seeking Peer Relationships

Developing a peer relationship with an intimate partner of the opposite gender is not always easy especially given the dominant socialization which women and men experience. Some even question whether it is possible for heterosexuals to have a peer relationship given the social, political, and economic differences in power between women and men. (At least here lesbians and gay men have somewhat of an advantage: the inequality of gender per se is absent and we have few models to limit us.) But it is possible for women and men to relate as peers in an intimate relationship *if* they openly acknowledge the reality of the social, political, and economic context in which they live and adjust accordingly. For example, because women generally still do not find equal pay for equal work, there might be a significant disparity between the incomes of the man and woman in a couple. In order to ameliorate this external disparity, the couple might decide to contribute an equal percentage to the common household fund. So if the man makes $35,000 per year and the woman makes $20,000 per year, each might contribute 35 percent of their income to the joint account. The amount of his contribution would be greater only because his income was greater, but they would be contributing equally. Or, because it is likely to be harder for a woman to find employment in her field, her job search would take priority and he would agree to follow her if a move were required. These kinds of considerations can help a couple deal with externally imposed inequities and lessen the impact on the parity of their relationship.

For gays and lesbians, the issues which mitigate against a peer relationship are more likely to be age and economic status, two factors which are often linked. For example, if two men are in a relationship and the older one is at mid career and the younger one just beginning his career, the implications of these realities must be addressed. If they agree that the older partner's career takes priority now and requires a geographical move, then they might also agree that ten years later the reverse will be true and as the younger partner reaches mid career, his job will determine where they live. A difference in age may also result in a difference in physical ability as the individuals age. So if at one time the couple enjoyed wilderness backpacking together, the older partner may reach a time when she is not able to continue that activity. The couple might decide to take up car camping instead or the younger partner may continue the activity with younger friends. All couples need to consider how they want to communicate in ways that support and sustain a peer relationship. This means each partner listens carefully and takes seriously the thoughts and feelings expressed by the other partner and tries to express his/her thoughts and feelings in return. This may be a challenge for the man who has not been socialized to listen to his partner. He may have to learn specific skills for listening and for sharing his thoughts and feelings.

Likewise, a couple can discuss ways they want to relate so that one person's physical size and strength will not be used in any way to intimidate their partner. This might mean both agreeing to remain seated during heated or conflictual discussions so that the larger person does not loom over the smaller person. If both persons in an intimate relationship are committed to relating as peers, methods such as this one acknowledge a predetermined difference in power and attempt to minimize its impact.

The point is to seek ways to insure that the differences between partners which often reflect differences in power and resources not become blocks to equality and shared decision-making in a peer relationship.

Those of us who carry a measure of social power and authority due to role, status, or age, in relation to those who have less social power for the same reasons (which means all adults vis-à-vis children), carry a special burden when considering initiating a sexual relationship. Even if we experience an attraction and desire for intimacy with someone who is in some way clearly less powerful than we are, we should avoid pursuing such a relationship. The teacher/student, therapist/client, minister/congregant, adult/child relationship is not a peer relationship. There is inevitably a difference in power between the two which precludes an authentically consenting relationship (see chapter 6, "Authentic Consent") These persons are off limits to our sexual interests.

Similarly, since most of us are in some way in relationship to our teacher, boss, therapist, or minister, where we have less power, we should not expect that person to enter into a intimate relationship with us, and we should understand when their answer to our initiative is "no." We should look for a peer with whom to initiate such a relationship.

Invariably, this is easier said than done. There are two primary reasons that I take a clear position on the issue of sexual and emotional intimacy with someone who is not our peer and whom we encounter in our professional role. First, it is inappropriate because it is always a situation of unequal power and thus carries the possibility of lack of authentic consent. Second, and equally important, is the fact that such a relationship carries a public dimension. Because the two persons generally met in their roles in a public setting (such as a congregation, workplace, or university), there are other people involved and affected by their potential intimate relationship. If a teacher dates a student, it affects his other students. At the very least, it raises a potential conflict of interest and likelihood of favoritism. Likewise, if a supervisor dates her supervisee, it always affects the dynamics of their shared workplace.

It may be possible in some cases (except when one of the individuals involved is a minor, or the relationship is one between therapist and client), for two people to address this lack of equality caused by role differences in much the same way that I have suggested couples deal with gender, age, and economic inequality. In other words, a couple can decide to change those factors which create the structural inequality so that they can pursue a peer relationship. In the case of professional role dynamics, the couple can decide to abandon their professional relationship and pursue only their personal, intimate relationship. This is always complicated and risky because the roles played in the professional relationship invariably affect the dynamics of the intimate relationship. Such a decision should be considered with great care because the loss of the professional relationship is not an insignificant matter.

For example, if a minister and congregant (who have not been in a pastoral counseling relationship) are considering moving from a ministerial relationship to a personal one, how shall they actualize this move? What if the congregant has been a member of this congregation for twelve years and the minister only just arrived? Should not the minister resign this position and seek other employment rather than deprive the congregant of his/her community of faith? This is certainly an option; the point is that redefining a professional relationship is never easy or cost-free for either party. A minister who was dealing with a congregant who expressed interest in an intimate relationship with him finally said to her: "You must realize that if we get involved intimately, you will be losing a very good minister and gaining a mediocre lover." This was the reality check she needed; she no longer pursued an intimate relationship with her minister.

Seeking a peer relationship in which to find sexual intimacy is the best insurance there is for avoiding abuse and for finding trust and fulfillment in relationship. Look for a partner who is your equal, who is a grown-up, who knows how to take care of him/herself, earns his/her own living, and is not threatened by your strengths and capabilities. Combine these attributes with common interests and sexual attraction, and you are well on your way to as healthy, pleasurable, satisfying relationship with "an equal, a companion, a familiar friend" as the psalmist described the loved one.

6 Authentic Consent

We went to the drive-in with Marion Eugene and Mustard. That boy is all hands. I have to keep eating candy and popcorn so he will leave me alone. After the movie they always want to go parking. Mustard and Pickle sit and smooch. Pickle says she doesn't like it but she will do anything, short of going all the way, to get a date to the Senior Prom. I am tired of fighting Marion Eugene off. Someone told him when a girl says no, she really means yes. I'd love to get hold of the person who started that one.

> —Daisy Fay in *Daisy Fay and the Miracle Man* by Fannie Flagg

Guideline #2. *Are both my partner and I authentically consenting to our sexual interaction? Both of us must have information, awareness, equal power and the option to say "no" without being punished, as well as the option to say "yes."*

∽ WHAT DOES CONSENT REALLY LOOK LIKE? According to the booklet, "Man-to-Man: When Your Partner Says *No*," consent is possible in a situation in which your partner:

- has "the right and ability to say yes or no to sexual contact *at any point*, without the threat of consequence or harm";
- must "be of legal age";
- must "be in a clear state of mind, not impaired (impairment includes being under the influence of drugs and/or

alcohol, experiencing mental illness/deficiency, develop-
mentally disabled, or being in any position where she is not
able to speak for herself, such as when sleeping or injured)";
- must "speak your language fluently enough to understand
fully what is being asked";
- must "be able to understand the potential consequences
of and alternatives to what is being asked."[1]

Although this booklet is addressed to heterosexual men, the suggestions it makes should concern all of us in relation to an intimate partner. Each of these factors serves to minimize
vulnerability, maximize equality and choice, and insure the benefits of a peer relationship. When written on paper, they may
sound legalistic. But in fact, they are common sense if we are concerned not to take advantage of our partner. Why would anyone
want to be sexual with someone under any other circumstances?

Authentic Consent?

The possibility of authentic consent presupposes a peer relationship
in which both persons have the capacity and resources to exercise
moral agency and choice. Authentic consent should not be confused with submission, the absence of non-consent, or acquiescence. Consent is often presumed when it is not present. For
instance, "choice" is a peculiar notion to someone who experiences
sex as something done to them by another person. That person will
most likely end up choosing among three options: being acted upon
(having sex); dealing with the consequences of saying "no" and not
being acted upon sexually; or saying "no" and being acted upon
anyway. She/he may well determine that acquiescing to unwanted
sex is less unpleasant than the consequences of saying "no."

Because of the norms of heterosexuality discussed earlier, many
men presume sexual access to women and so may engage in a
process of persuasion in complete disregard for authentic consent.
These dynamics may also appear in same-sex relationships. One

teenage girl observed: "I guess in all three relationships, there was a lot of forcing me sexually into doing what I didn't want to do. I'd do it just to get them off my back . . . basically I felt if I didn't, then I'd have to deal with him for the next couple of days making me feel bad . . . and it's . . . not worth the hassle. Go along with it and play the game."[2] Or as another woman explained:

> Well I wasn't raped, raped, because I did—I—See, I've actually never been raped, but I mean really it's a fine line, isn't it, between saying yes, whether you want to or not, to somebody like that, that I didn't really want to go to bed with. Ah, I've I mean I suppose I've been sort of pushed around but, but not hurt. Just manhandled but not violently. . . . . He, he didn't rape me, because I really more or less consented. . . . I acquiesced, in my actions, but not my words. I didn't say 'oh, okay,' I just let him get on with it.[3]

Neither of these women authentically consented, that is, freely chose to be sexual with their partners. Both found their choices severely limited because their partners had no respect for their lack of consent.

In another example, a woman named Chloe acquiesced to avoid the inevitable argument which would ensue if she said "no": "And, um, really getting, like getting into major arguments because I didn't want to have sex. Like, that—not actually being forced to have sex, but sometimes saying yes when I didn't really want to. . . . And the argument standing out as the most unpleasant thing. Things like actually being called a fucking bitch and having the door slammed. And trying always to explain that it didn't mean that I didn't care because I didn't want to have sex, but never succeeding."[4] It was just easier to acquiesce to her partner's initiative than to resist. "No" was not a real option. But many women in Chloe's situation get confused and start believing that *caring about* or *loving* their partner means acquiescing to sexual activity they don't really want.

Some women minimize the meaning of sexual contact in order to tolerate their ambivalence. Take Pat's experience: "I have often gone to bed with him when I haven't really wanted to, when I haven't felt that I wanted to. . . . what you do is, you simply, um, suppress your own needs, because what he wants is to go to bed with you and you tell yourself it really doesn't matter much either way."[5] Or Lee's experience of what she would say to herself when her lover was pressuring her to have sex: "One was that, um, oh, why don't you just say 'yes', I mean it's it's a nothing—it's like, having sex is like getting up and having breakfast. . . . I think in a way that . . . was a way of making it, making the *ordinariness* of it okay. I think it was just ordinary, it is just like having a cup of tea."[6] These are experiences of pragmatic acquiescence to a partner's sexual pressure. But they are not experiences of authentic consent. At no point did these women have the chance to consider *their* desire or interest in sexual activity.

These assumptions about what constitutes consent—primarily made about women—are particularly problematic when it comes to understanding women's moral agency. In 1992, a woman brought a charge of rape against a stranger who broke into her apartment, held her at knife point, and raped her. Before he raped her, she asked the rapist to please wear a condom (which she provided). He agreed. The first Grand Jury that was impanelled refused to indict the man because he argued that since she asked him to wear a condom, she was consenting. This judicial situation reveals the legal and moral vacuum that exists regarding authentic consent. (Subsequent to the outraged public response, the prosecutor refiled the case, and the man was indicted, prosecuted, and convicted.)[7]

The initial refusal to indict this man was an indicator that the Grand Jury regarded the woman's act of requesting that the man wear a condom in order to protect her from disease and pregnancy as a sign of her consent to have sex with him. Her acting as a moral agent to protect herself as much as possible from a man holding a knife at her throat was interpreted as consent. "If she didn't want to have sex with me, why did she ask me to wear a condom?" To save her life, obviously. In fact what was going on here was that any agency at all on her part rendered her no longer an "innocent victim" in the eyes of the Grand Jury. She then is not only consenting, she is culpable for *his* actions. (No doubt the fact that she possessed a condom in the first place indicated to the Grand Jury that she was a sexually active adult woman, which rendered her "unrapable" in their eyes.) What is confusing in our current moral climate is that any moral agency by a woman is viewed then as total responsibility for the situation.

The absence of physical coercion should not be equated with the presence of authentic consent. And yet many times it is. Defense attorneys often make these arguments on behalf of accused rapists: "she agreed to have sex with me" (after he put a gun to her head); "she didn't say 'no'"; "there was no physical struggle, no marks on her body." These are all variations on the adage, "you can't thread a moving needle." In other words, it's impossible to have sex with someone who does not want to have sex. A 1994 ruling in the Pennsylvania Supreme Court presents this as a legal standard. The ruling states that unless the victim physically resisted (which usually means can show evidence of physical injury), it was not rape. In other words, her verbal indication of "no" is insufficient and thus becomes irrelevant.[8] The vagaries of judicial decision-making often reveal an inability to view rape from the perspective of the victim. Lack of consent, although indicated, is ignored.

Some who promote sadomasochism argue that consent is very real between the sadist and the masochist, that the masochist agrees to everything the sadist does to her/him. But some who have lived through the experience disagree. A battered woman who went to a shelter shared her experience of being forced by her husband to use violent pornography and to participate in s/m practices including bondage. Because her frame of reference and information was quite limited, she assumed that all husbands required these things of their wives and that she had no real choice in the matter. She was surprised to learn differently from other women at the shelter. Another woman shared this experience:

> Sadomasochism was a part of the abuse I endured in a recent lesbian relationship . . . Sadomasochism, in my experience, has nothing to do with love. It is the externalization of self-hatred poured onto another woman's body . . . My experience shows me that sadomasochism's involvement of an imbalance of power leads to an inherent tendency towards abuse of another's vulnerability. The pretense of consent and free choice advocated among sadomasochists does not account for the intimidation that one person can exert in that type of relationship.[9]

A dominant/submissive relationship or interaction precludes authentic consent.

Even in what one presumes is a peer relationship, lack of authentic consent can occur. After a presentation to a church youth group, I was approached by a sixteen-year-old girl wanting to tell her story. She said that she had been going steady with a sixteen-year-old boy for six months. She really liked him, enjoyed his company, shared common interests with him, etc. He told her that he wanted to have sex with her. She replied that she did not want to have sex with him for a variety of reasons beginning with the fact that she didn't feel ready. He did not force her sexually as he might have (given that date rape is an alarmingly common occurrence among teenagers). Instead he ended the relationship. He was basically saying, "either have sex with me or lose me." This was coercion. He was punishing her for saying "no." Her "no" was not a real option; this was not a relationship in which the boyfriend valued consent.

In reflecting on this experience, the girl indicated that she was glad that the relationship had ended. She did not want to be in a relationship with anyone who would not respect her choices, especially about sexual activity. But she had not wanted the relationship to end. She was saying "no" to sexual activity, not to the relationship. She exercised her moral agency in spite of consequences which she would otherwise not have chosen.

"What Is it About 'No' That You Don't Understand?"

This has become the standard retort to the infuriating comment from men whose workplace misconduct is confronted directly: "I don't understand what you mean by 'no.'" Men's effort to minimize their responsibility combined with the cliche "women say 'no' when they mean 'yes'" has set the stage for a good deal of confusion, miscommunication, and perhaps unintended abuse. Of course the dilemma which it creates for women is clear: if "no" means "yes," what is the word for "no?" When it comes to communication about sexual interaction, some people behave as if there is a different language. Both women and men learn this "romance" language. In fact, they are instructed in it by professionals. *The Intimate Enemy—How to Fight Fair in Love and Marriage*, first published in 1969, is a book still being used by some therapists. The authors, Bach and Wyden, suggest the following:

> When [women] say "no, not now," they really mean "Yes if" (you really passionately want me). Then such a wife can give herself to the rapist [her husband] and say "I'm overcome by you." . . . Men should not simply assume that their partners don't at times feel like being raped; and that 'no' can mean 'yes' if the pursuit is persistent, skillful and genuinely passionate.[10]

The notion of authentic consent easily becomes lost in this kind of socialization which legitimizes the dominant/submissive sexual relationship.

Most of the time, women say "no" when they mean no. But their "no" doesn't carry any meaning because there doesn't seem to be a word for "no" in this peculiar language. In an interview, Ann made this observation: ". . . it's partly having the language to say no. Like, this sort of amorphous feeling of, 'Ooh, I'm not sure about this,' but having the language to say it, and, and, and also I guess, feeling that if you said it, it would have any effect. Because there is always that fear that you could say no and it [sic] would carry on anyway, and, and being physically less, and then you'd be raped sort of thing, and then it would be terrible."[11] Ann is struggling with two critical aspects of her sexual relationship. First, although she doesn't really want to have sex in this situation, she worries that her "no" would not work. She is confronting the reality that she does not have the power in this relationship to say "no" and have her wishes respected by her partner. Second, although Ann's feelings may have ranged from strong ambivalence to not wanting to be sexual with her partner, she believed that the fact that she did not say "no" meant that she was consenting and therefore the experience was not rape which meant it would not be so "terrible." In other words, she was playing mind games with herself in order to make the experience less traumatic than it was. But she was not consenting; she was compliant. Her "choice" not to say "no" was made in the context of a non-consensual interaction in which her moral agency was limited. Her choice was between forced sex to which she submitted or forced sex which she resisted. This is no real choice at all in a relationship in which consent is not valued.

Each of these women experienced "pressured sex." Pressured sex includes these tactics from sexual partners: nagging, begging, lying, false promises, guilt-tripping, emotional blackmail, pinching, grabbing, etc. as well as "manhandling," violence, threat of a weapon, etc.[12] Extreme jealousy is also a means by which a partner seeks to control the other. Jealousy is not a sign of love; jealousy is a sign of control. These tactics make no pretense of a consenting relationship.

The supposed confusion about the meaning of consent is not limited to sexual experiences. A news article with the title, "'Lovesick' Official Accused of Stalking" tells the story:

> A 'lovesick' Riverdale city councilman has resigned after he was accused in a warrant of stalking a Clayton County businesswoman for more than a month. Councilman Ralph

Thomas, 63, said Friday he is *in love* [italics mine] with Betty McRae of Morrow, who charged in the warrant that he stalked her after their six-month relationship went sour. . . . The two met through a mutual friend and went dancing and to the movies, Ms. McRae said, but he apparently couldn't accept her decision when she called it quits. Saying she begged Mr. Thomas to leave her alone, Ms. McRae told of harassing phone calls at all hours of the day and night—sometimes as many as 15 or 16 an hour—over the past six weeks. . . . Ms. McRae said she became fearful when she found notes Mr. Thomas allegedly had left on her car stating: 'I can't live without you' and 'Why did you turn on me?' . . . Mr. Thomas said he had no idea the couple's relationship had *gone sour* [italics mine] until the warrant was issued for his arrest.[13]

While this is clearly a case of stalking and harassment, it is not recognized as such by the perpetrator or by a significant portion of the community. The stalker is excused by the newspaper article as being "lovesick," meaning he "can't help himself" and is not seen as responsible for his actions.

Recognition of the often deadly consequences of stalking and harassment by men whose romantic advances have been rebuffed has finally led to some statutory protection for women. Contrary to the image portrayed in the movie *Fatal Attraction* of the crazed single woman who wouldn't take "no" for an answer from her married lover, most stalking and harassment is carried out by men against women.* Martha R. Mahoney, a law professor, uses the term "separation assault" to describe the response of some batterers to their partners leaving them:

Separation assault is the attack on the woman's body and volition in which her partner seeks to prevent her from leaving,

---

* The City Attorney's Office in Seattle, WA, where there is a statute against harassment, reports that they typically receive 100 complaints of harassment per month. Fewer than one percent of that 100 per month involve a female harassing a male; 99 percent are men harassing women.

retaliate for the separation, or force her to return. It aims at overbearing her will as to where and with whom she will live, and coercing her in order to enforce connection in a relationship. It is an attempt to gain, retain, or regain power in a relationship, or to punish the woman for ending the relationship. It often takes place over time.[14]

Why would someone pursue a relationship with a person who is clearly not consenting? Because what that person is seeking is not a consenting relationship but a relationship in which he can control his partner in complete disregard of her lack of consent. This behavior is called "battering" and it can occur in any type of intimate relationship.

When "No" Means "Yes"

Let's acknowledge that some women do say "no" to a partner's sexual initiative when they mean "yes" because they don't know or feel comfortable with "yes" to sexual activity. This hesitation and confusion can be the result of one of two things: many women have been socialized to believe that sexual activity is dirty and sinful and have been given very little information about female sexuality. They have probably also been taught that the only thing men are interested in is sex and that their task as women is to defend their chastity against this onslaught of male hormones. Regardless of their sexual feelings, regardless of their desires, and regardless of the effectiveness of their "no," women have long been taught to say "no" to men's sexual advances. (Moreover, in the era which preceded effective contraception, this defense was the only protection against pregnancy.) For women who learned this lesson, there was no word for "yes" in their vocabulary. The women who did learn the secret of the word "yes" often lived with the consequences of enormous guilt and, in some cases, unwanted pregnancy. Although the availability of contraception and sex education have helped many women learn the word "yes" and feel comfortable using it, for many others, cultural norms and religious teachings still preclude the word "yes" from their sexual vocabulary which makes communication about consent with a partner very difficult.

Another reason for hesitancy or confusion about "yes" and "no" for either women or men may be a person's history of sexual abuse. Experiencing sexual abuse as a child or teenager dramatically shapes the development of one's sexual self.[15] It may inhibit sexual openness because of the damage done to trust and because of the fear of intimate interaction. "Women who have been molested often feel tension for the rest of their lives in certain areas of the body and mind, and often cannot experience sexual arousal without a mixture of tension and fear."[16] Since at least one-third of all females are introduced to sex by being molested by a "trusted" family member,[17] it should come as no surprise that confusion, hesitation, and ambivalence about sexual activity are common in women's experiences. While some men may experience confusion and ambivalence as a result of childhood abuse, they are more likely than women to feel anger and to abuse others as a result:

> Physical or sexual abuse in childhood may result in displaced anger that is expressed sexually against a partner because of a need to feel powerful and in control. Some victims of childhood abuse learn that being abusive is 'normal' or 'okay,' or that it is a way not to be victimized again.[18]

Once again this residue from childhood sexual abuse can show up in same-sex relationships as well as heterosexual relationships.

When "Yes" Means "No"

Ironically, this same history of sexual abuse may encourage someone to say "yes" when they mean "no." For the survivor of sexual abuse who was taught that they have no personal boundaries, that their self-worth as a person is a function of their sexual attractiveness and availability to anyone who would have them, there is no word for "no" in their vocabulary. Their indiscriminate sexual activity is then viewed by outsiders as "promiscuous" and its reasons never inquired into. Tragically, many young adults have not come to terms with their childhood sexual abuse and thus may find it difficult to comprehend their own patterns of sexual activity.

"Yes, Yes" and Then "No"

Some people complain that their partner says "yes, yes" to their sexual initiatives up to a point and then says "no." This is unfair, they say. One "yes" should be good for the whole evening at least, if not for the whole relationship. In an interview, a woman named Pat said this: "There've been times in my life when I have really felt like . . . 'What the hell did I go to bed with that man for? Why am I doing this, I must be mad. Why can't I say no?,' you know. . . . If you've been to bed with them once, then there's no reason why, that you shouldn't go to bed with them again in their heads. And of course [pause], I mean, you can see that point of view [laughing]."[19] Of course Pat realizes the contradiction in what she is saying. The logic is only logical to someone for whom authentic consent to sexual activity is not a value.

These circumstances seem ludicrous when compared to other human interactions. Someone may say "yes, I want to test drive the car"; "yes, I want to buy the car"; yes, here is the down payment on the car"; "no thanks, I've changed my mind." This is perfectly acceptable. Why is it less acceptable to change one's mind about sexual interaction? The key here is communication and an agreement that changing one's mind is always an option. With this as a given, it is our responsibility to be as clear as we possibly can be about our openness or lack of openness to sexual activity with our partner at every point in our interaction. Likewise, it is our responsibility to listen carefully to our partner and respect "no" when we hear it.

So What Does Authentic Consent Look Like?

One partner may initiate sexual activity, and this initiative may be verbal or non-verbal. The responding partner then should have a real option to participate or not. (The initiating and responding roles alternate between sex partners depending on mood, desire, and the like. No one partner should always be expected to initiate sexual contact.) If she/he chooses not to be sexual at that moment in time, for whatever reason, there may be consequences: for example, the initiating partner may be disappointed and may not be available when the other partner is interested later on. But these real consequences are not the stuff of emotional blackmail. They are simply realities that both should be able to live with.

The responding partner has a range of options in response. He/she may not be particularly aroused and eager for sexual activity, but may be very comfortable participating as a way of giving to his/her partner. The experience is not unpleasant but neither is it one which that partner would have initiated him/herself. Or the responding partner may be equally aroused in response to her/his partner's initiative and so the exchange of pleasure and affection becomes mutual and shared, providing both physical release and emotional fulfillment.

This is Alicia's experience: "I would come home from work and start dinner. Sometimes when I knew that she had had a hard day at work, I would run a hot tub just when I expected her home. When she got there, I would suggest the tub and some fun before dinner. Sometimes this was just what she needed; other times not. Either way we had a good soak and a good dinner."

Or consider Tom's experience: "If I have been gone on a business trip, she usually waits up for me. When we get into bed, she wants to be close and intimate because she missed me. I am usually just exhausted from travel. So sometimes when she wants to be sexual, I say 'no.' Then we usually cuddle and talk in bed and wait until we are both more rested to be more sexual. It used to hurt her feelings but she has come to understand what my 'no' means."

The dynamic of sexual interaction should be one of giving and receiving between two people. This experience within a context of intimacy, safety and trust can create bonds between people which are emotionally meaningful. There are certainly times when a couple may decide to compromise:

> Compromise involves a mutual, consensual decision to yield on some issues and not on others, and involves modifying beliefs and values. Neither participant *gives up* values or beliefs; both agree to engage in specified behaviors. Compromise requires that both people have a choice, both have power in the decision-making process, and both are equal.[20]

If we are truly concerned to insure that our partner is authentically consenting, if we truly respect our partner's choice, then we must be always open to hear that their "yes" has changed to "no." No explanation is needed. We do not need to talk them into anything. "No" means no. There are certainly times when we or our partner may be confused, uncertain, or unclear about our sexual interest. This is especially difficult at times for survivors of sexual abuse who are struggling with intimacy, trust, and sexual interaction. Here a patient partner can be very helpful. Sometimes the prudent action is no action.

For example, Rod and Don are entering a new and monogamous relationship. Don has been very sexually active for several years. Rod has not been active for about two years but was very active prior to that time. Both have histories of childhood sexual abuse. Don wanted sexual intimacy in their relationship right away. Rod expressed his need for emotional security and a sense of physical safety within the relationship before relating genitally. Don understood Rod's "no" and together they have created a framework of progression toward sexual intimacy, including both being tested for HIV. They even established groundrules for sleeping together before sex; they cuddle and kiss but go no further until both feel ready. Don is actually enjoying this way of experiencing growth in a relationship. And Rod feels his needs are being honored.

In these passages from "Checkpoint: A Lover's Game,"

Kathleen Fleming describes the sexual interaction between two women who have come up with a way of communicating "yes, no or maybe" in the midst of their sexual activity and in the context of their individual histories and memories. She refers to "points" as a way of communicating affirmation and "checkpoint" as the signal for interrupting specific activity.

> If your mouth has moved lightly from breast to breast and found its way down my arm, past the flickering of passion on the inside of my palm, to thigh and thigh again, and then to opening thighs and the place within that is like a hidden stream that murmurs under moss, and you move your tongue in a joyous, first gentle, then wild rhythmic thrust. . . .

> If your mouth has moved lightly from breast to breast and found its way down my arm, past the flickering of passion on the inside of my palm, to thigh and thigh again, and then to opening thighs and the place within that is like a hidden stream that murmurs under moss, and you move your tongue in a motion that is hard and harder like his beat. . . .

> If I whisper "Checkpoint" you will pause, kiss my thigh, my arm, my shoulder, take my head against your shoulder, and wait until I turn again to kiss. . . .

> and I will have thirty points for saying no even though I knew you were deep into your pleasure, even though I knew I'd welcomed you, even though I was afraid you'd think I meant a different, larger no.

> * * *

> If I am sitting with you watching television and I put my arms around you, touching your breasts with my curved palms the way I would touch water in a mountain stream, thinking to bend to put my lips there soon, to suck in the sweet fresh water gathered in my cool cupped hands. . . .

If I am sitting with you watching television and I put my arms around you, touching your breasts with my curved palms the way I would touch water in a mountain stream, thinking to bend to put my lips there soon, to suck in the sweet water gathered in my hands that for you are huge and glossy against your tiny breasts, that chafe as against concrete when you skin your knee. . . .

if you say, "Checkpoint," I will stand and stretch, go for popcorn, and remember that circling you from behind that way is not okay, for which I get ten points.

and you will have thirty points for interrupting such sweet pleasure as we both might have had even though you're wide awake and could persuade yourself that it would have been okay.

* * *

If you glide across my lips, arms, breasts like an evening breeze and I am wild with desire for your tongue and you lay your cheek against my thigh and with your fingers find a path your tongue will follow, expecting me to rise and rise with you . .

If you glide across my lips, arms, breasts like an evening breeze and I am wild with desire for your tongue and you lay your cheek against my thigh and with your fingers find a path your tongue will follow, trapping me to holding still beneath your weighted touch. . . .

If I allow myself to breathe and watch your face that I find beautiful, and I feel your hand as yours, as loving touch, and know I can lift two fingers any time and in an instant the touch will pause, and if I then stay with delight and claim my own desire as my own and I stay with you as your desire and mine conspire to delight. . . .

If I do that I don't need points: I'll settle for delight.[21]

Methods such as these are available to adult peers in any intimate relationship who value consent, who respect each other, and who desire to know the trust and intimacy which authentic consent can bring. The reward is well worth the effort.

It is time I want with you, my love, day after day. I want us to walk beside the lake for many hours, day after day, with only your hand in mine, my hand in yours, to signal our hearts' intent.

I want time in which to know we can take forever if we want before we kiss and forever after that to stroke and touch and kiss again.

It is time I want with you, my love, day after day.

It is time I want with you until you know my voice is mine, until I know your touch is yours, until you know the morning light belongs to you and me, until I know my body mine to sometimes meet with yours in love, until you know your spirit is as free as any hawk's, to light near me when that is your heart's choice and to soar alone and high when that is your heart's choice, as I will soar at will when I have need.[22]

7 Stewardship of My Sexuality

I call heaven and earth to witness against you today that I have set before you life and death, blessings and curses. Choose life so that you and your descendants may live, . . .

—Deuteronomy 30:19 NRSV

The choice to protect oneself [from HIV infection] requires three things: knowledge, positive self-regard, and accessibility to the means of protection.

—*Affirming Persons–Saving Lives*

Guideline #3. *Do I take responsibility for protecting myself and my partner against sexually transmitted diseases and to insure reproductive choice? This is a question of stewardship (the wise care for and management of the gift of sexuality) and anticipating the literal consequences of our actions. Taking this responsibility seriously presupposes a relationship: knowing someone over time and sharing a history in which trust can develop.*

✂ THIS CHAPTER WOULD HAVE BEEN written differently in the late 1970s. But now we are all living with the reality of AIDS which lends a particular urgency to any discussion of ethical responsibility in a sexual relationship. Responsible sexual behavior is now a matter of life and death. We are also living in a time when the right wing continues its attack on reproductive choice which often stifles education about and availability of safe, reliable contraception. Once again the potential forums for discussion of ethics as it relates to responsible sexual behavior are, by and large, strangely silent.

Safer Sex?

If we consider the ethical question of responsibility for safer sex (and reproductive choice) from the starting point of Paul's biblical assertion that "love does no wrong to a neighbor" or our commitment to "do least harm" to the other person, our responsibility seems clear. I am responsible for protecting my partner and myself from sexually transmitted diseases. If I know that I am infected with HIV or have been diagnosed with AIDS, and I engage in unprotected sexual activity or do not inform my partner of my condition, it is no different than if I knowingly prepare a meal with food contaminated with botulism toxin and invite my partner to eat it. By and large the community response has been to minimize information about HIV and AIDS, especially to young people, and simply to urge sexual abstinence.* In the absence of a strong, sensible ethical mandate in the wider community, the law is making our responsibility clear. In more than half the states in the United States, it is illegal for a person with HIV to have sex without telling his/her partner. In some states, knowingly exposing a person to HIV is criminal and prosecuted as second-degree assault.[1] While this is not the complete answer to the problem, legislatures are filling a vacuum by attempting to link behavior and consequences.

---

* This statement is in no way intended to overlook the excellent work that many community agencies have done to provide information about safer sex particularly in the gay community and in communities of color. In the gay community, workshops and support groups help participants learn new ways of courtship and how to discuss sexual histories and values. To reach smaller, isolated communities, computer networks are helping to share information and teach new social skills. But the wider community still hesitates to use its resources to educate adequately about HIV and AIDS.

If I am unwilling to consider that my conduct could put my partner at risk for potentially life threatening disease, then I am in fundamental denial that there are consequences to my actions. This was the case for basketball star, Magic Johnson. In late 1992, he was sued by a former lover who alleged that he infected her with the AIDS virus. At the time he had sex with this woman, he did not know that he was infected with HIV. Is he liable? Her lawsuit argues that he should have known, ". . . that his ignorance was willful and his behavior wantonly dangerous. . . . In his book he writes, 'In the age of AIDS, unprotected sex is reckless. I know that now, of course. But the truth is, I knew it then, too. I just didn't pay attention.'"[2] His sexual partner asked him to use a condom before intercourse; Johnson refused. He was irresponsible; his conduct was life-threatening. Although it was clearly his responsibility at this point, hopefully she also had a choice (if we assume an authentically consenting relationship): to refuse to have unprotected sex with him. If she had the option to withhold her consent in this relationship, then it was her responsibility to do whatever she could to protect herself.

It is more true than ever before that having sex with someone is equivalent to having sex with every one of that person's previous partners. This is not a decision to be made lightly, under the influence of alcohol or drugs, or on the spur of the moment. It is a decision best made in the context of a relationship which is built over time and in which trust and communication are priorities. If your partner is impatient with your wanting to build this relationship slowly, you may want to look elsewhere for a partner.

Unfortunately, when it comes to protection against disease (and against unwanted pregnancy), women in relationships with men are physiologically at a disadvantage. Women are the only ones who can get pregnant by having sex with men, and women are more likely to be infected by HIV from sex with men than vice versa.[3] In addition, women in a patriarchal culture and a male-dominated relationship often find that their choices and their moral agency are limited in matters of contraception and prevention of STDs (sexually transmitted diseases). The announcement in early 1993 of a new contraceptive device for women, a "female condom," was greeted with little enthusiasm by commentator Cynthia Tucker:

> The makers of this device proclaim its advantages: It will allow women at least minimal protection from pregnancy and sexually transmitted diseases if they are involved with men who refuse to wear condoms themselves. The most revealing endorsement of this new device come from female physicians who have among their patients women whose husbands are infected with the virus that causes AIDS. Those doctors say some women are reluctant or powerless to insist their infected husbands wear condoms.... This new gadget is ... a dubious salve for relationships with very deep wounds. What kind of love is it when an HIV-infected husband refuses to wear a condom for his wife? And what kind of relationship is it if she is afraid to insist?[4]

Tucker is asking the important ethical questions here and pointing to the very real circumstances that many women face. In some of these instances, the woman's moral agency and options are virtually nonexistent because of the threat of violence by her partner. According to the National Centers for Disease Control, there is a link between battering and the spread of HIV among women. Many battered women have been infected with HIV by batterers who forced their partners into unprotected sex, with the intent of discouraging them from having sex with other men.[5]

Finally, you may be faced with the question: "what am I doing in a relationship in which my partner does not even respect me enough to want to protect me from a life-threatening disease?" In this case, it is your job to protect yourself: this may mean leaving such a relationship.

Hearing about and being encouraged to protect yourself against HIV infection may be difficult if you are a victim or survivor of sexual abuse. Some victims or survivors engage in behaviors which they have learned as coping mechanisms for the pain of past experiences. Cathy Kidman's research on HIV education is revealing:

> For example, alcohol and drugs may be used to numb the reality of what happened or is currently happening, and can be a protective behavior against suicide or self-mutilation. One HIV-positive survivor told me that exchanging sex for money gave her the feeling of control over her body, and at that time in her life, she remembers feeling that her self-esteem increased. In her words, 'It was better than either giving it away or having it taken. I felt like my body was worth something.'[6]

Finally, only you can protect yourself by refusing to engage in risky sexual behavior. If you are having difficulty standing up for yourself and saying "no" to risky sex, find someone to talk to about it who can help you understand why and can support you in saying "no."

Reproductive Choice

If you are in a heterosexual relationship in which your partner or you could get pregnant as a result of your sexual activity, then you each have a responsibility to insure that you choose together whether or not to exercise your reproductive capability. To take this responsibility seriously is to do least harm to your partner, yourself, and to the child who might be born as a result of your sexual activity. Ideally, you should discuss whether or not you want to have a child at this time in your lives and in your relationship. If not, you should discuss what contraceptive methods you will use, considering potential side effects and failure rates. You should discuss how you each feel about the possibility of an unwanted pregnancy and what you would do about it. If you decide that because of your age, circumstances, or personal choices that you no longer want the option to father or to bear children, then you should seek out a safe means of sterilization for yourself.

Women should be able to choose whether or not they become pregnant. They should have the option to exercise their moral agency in this matter which means that they should not be forced to engage in any sexual activity they don't choose and that, if they choose to be sexual with a man, they should have information and safe contraception readily available to them. All of this presupposes ideal circumstances. In a less than ideal situation, if you are involved with a partner who refuses to share responsibility for reproductive choice, then you must take on that responsibility alone, whether you are male or female. You should use the contraceptive that is safest for you and over which you have the most control.

If a woman becomes pregnant due to contraceptive failure, rape, carelessness, irresponsibility, or any other means that denies her choice, she is then faced with an unwanted pregnancy. Regardless of the circumstance, she must exercise her moral agency to choose whether or not to carry the fetus to term. She should be able to make this choice privately and, if she so desires, in consultation with her doctor, family, and supportive religious leader based on her values and beliefs. In order to make a moral choice, options must be available to her. This is why a woman's right to choose abortion should not be denied by the government. The choice to have an abortion is often complex for a woman who feels a moral responsibility to choose based on her life circumstances. There are times in a woman's life when, in spite of her best attempts, contraceptives fail and the economics or stability of her relationship make it impossible to have a child and care for it responsibly. When a woman is made pregnant by rape or incest, the anguish and pain of having the child of one's assailant is very often too great to bear. When there is a significant likelihood that a fetus is severely deformed, it may be impossible for a family or community to adequately care for the child. Women in these circumstances may face difficult choices and deserve the support and understanding of their family, friends, and religious community as they work through their decisions. The choice to terminate a pregnancy can be a choice to do least harm.

Being able to take responsibility to protect oneself against disease or unwanted pregnancy requires a sense of self that is worth protecting *and* a partner who is trustworthy. Developing trust in one's partner can only happen over time. This is the best argument against one-night-stands with a stranger. Basically, such one-night-stands are stupid and dangerous. Having sex with someone you just met means having sex with someone who may be violent, who may have a sexually transmitted disease, and who may be untrustworthy and irresponsible. Why take that chance?

Moral Discernment in a Wider Context

Where are the voices from the religious community in response to these hard questions? The loudest voices come from the religious right who oppose abortion, contraception, condom distribution, and AIDS education, and would deny women's moral agency in any of these matters. The few helpful voices come mostly from the margins: feminist, gay, and lesbian religious leaders. Within the mainline Protestant denominations and Reform Judaism, there are strong (but nonetheless marginal) voices urging and offering resources to help people deal with difficult ethical issues regarding sexuality.* The Roman Catholic Church vociferously represents the conservative position (shared by many fundamentalist Christians) by maintaining official teachings which prohibit the use of artificial contraception, condoms even for safer sex, and abortion. How supposedly responsible church leaders can persist in

---

* See recent reports from United Methodist, Presbyterian Church (U.S.A.), Evangelical Lutheran Church in America and others; also see curricula from the United Church of Christ and Unitarian Universalist Association, especially *Affirming Persons–Saving Lives* from the United Church of Christ, 700 Prospect St., Cleveland, Ohio 44115; other groups such as Catholics for a Free Choice and the Religious Coalition for Reproductive Choice are important voices in this discussion.

these contradictory teachings in the face of the worldwide AIDS epidemic and overpopulation remains incomprehensible and has deadly consequences.

Consider these situations:

A husband and wife gave birth to a baby who died shortly after birth from a genetic birth defect. As a result the parents discovered that they both carried the gene and that any subsequent pregnancy would produce a child who could not survive. These parents were Roman Catholic. The wife was particularly staunch in her practice of the faith. So the couple went to their parish priest for counsel.

The husband pleaded for permission to use artificial birth control so that they could have sex but not risk another pregnancy. Natural family planning had failed them. He wanted a vasectomy. The wife was very upset by his request. She knew it was contrary to church teaching. The priest, who was sensitive and genuinely troubled by their situation, could do nothing but repeat the church's prohibition against so-called artificial birth control including vasectomies and tubal ligations (based on the papal encyclical *Humanae Vitae*).

These two people loved each other very much and for both, their sexual relationship was an integral part of their love. Because of their genetic makeup, it would have been irresponsible for them to have sex without reliable contraception which could lead to the birth of more babies who would die quickly. Yet the rules of the Roman Catholic Church prevented them from using the contraception they needed. The stress and conflict which this situation created for this couple finally resulted in their separation and an annulment of their marriage. Their relationship was destroyed by the rules of the church.[7] How would the mandate to "do least harm" change the ethical discernment of this couple?

In another situation, a man who contracted the HIV virus from a blood transfusion was in a monogamous marriage. He went to his priest to ask permission to use a condom during sexual intercourse to protect his wife from the disease. The priest prohibited him from doing so. This couple was also left with no responsible option because of the rules of the church. They left the church, deeply disillusioned by its teaching.

These examples of rule-based ethics, unconnected to consequences or to the concern for doing least harm to one's neighbor, are only one indicator of the profound failure of many official religious teachings which ignore the very real and immediate ethical dilemmas of our day. If I am concerned to do least harm to my sexual partner, then I have to be concerned about the literal consequences of our sexual activity. I must exercise the same caution in this area of my life which I would in other areas. For example, I may enjoy driving a sports car at excessive speeds. But I cannot do so without endangering myself, my companion, or other drivers. So my desire to prevent harm to myself, my companion, and others, takes precedence over my desire to drive my sports car fast.

If I am to exercise my moral agency and make careful choices about my sexual activity, I require the following:

1. Information about sexually transmitted diseases and reproduction. Accurate, up-to-date information is more readily available than ever; but I must read, listen, and pay attention if I am to benefit from it.
2. Access to the material means to exercise my moral options. This means access to condoms and all forms of contraception as well as access to the option of abortion regardless of my financial means.
3. Communication with my partner. We need to discuss these issues *before the fact, not during the act.* We need to talk about our likes and dislikes, the relative risks of each contraceptive method, our sexual histories, the results of any tests we may have had for HIV or other STDs. In other words, we need to know each other well before we can make good decisions about safer sex.

In a perfect world, we would not even have to worry about these issues. In a perfect world, teen pregnancy would not be a problem. The AIDS epidemic would have been stopped before it got started. No one would get pregnant unless they want to bear and raise a child. Since we don't live in a perfect world, we are each faced with decisions and choices which profoundly affect us and others as well. Some among us are faced with these decisions and choices at an age when knowledge is scarce and maturity and wisdom are not yet well-developed.

Public Policy That Does Least Harm

In the United States, AIDS, contraception, and abortion are perhaps the most volatile political issues of our time. Efforts to prevent sexually transmitted diseases and unwanted pregnancy raise serious questions and confront not only our religious institutions but also public policy. It is up to public policy makers to insure that our right to privacy and choice is not denied by the government at the same time that the well-being of the common good is insured.

For example, the public policy discussion continues over whether or not sexuality education should be offered in public schools. Those who argue against sex education say that giving young people information will encourage sexual activity. In order to discourage activity, they reason, we should encourage their ignorance about sexuality. The fact is that young people get a lot of information about sexual activity every day. Most of it comes from highly questionable sources: the media and their peers. So the issue is not information versus no information, but rather, what the source of their information will be. We are much more likely to be able to have an impact on their decision making if we give them accurate information and help them learn to be responsible decision-makers. This is the responsibility of the school, the family, *and* religious institutions. School boards in particular need community support to press ahead with human sexuality curricula in spite of the vocal opposition from a small minority of parents.

Many teenagers today are sexually active: "Today more than half of all high school students are having sexual intercourse, and about one million teenagers—12 percent of all fifteen- to nineteen-year-olds—are getting pregnant each year."[8] But we must put these figures in context: "some 74 percent of women who had intercourse before age fourteen and 60 percent of those who had sex before age 15 report having had sex involuntarily."[9] In addition, among 19 percent of young women between the ages of fifteen to nineteen who become mothers, the father was at least six years older.[10] In these circumstances, the likelihood of coercion is high (see chapter 6, "Authentic Consent"). In studying young women who became pregnant during adolescence, researchers Boyer and Fine found that of those interviewed, "two thirds had been raped or sexually abused, nearly always by fathers, stepfathers, or other relatives or guardians."[11] So if we are serious about teenage sexual activity and pregnancy, we must be willing to address sexual abuse. As Sue Woodman argues, "The agenda should be not to blame girls but to fight against sexual predators, violence and incest at home, and a merchandising ethos that capitalizes on sex."[12]

In fact, some teenagers do abstain (or manage to avoid coercive sex) until adulthood or until they choose a partner in a committed relayionship such as marriage.[13] I would prefer that they abstain until they are old enough to make fully informed ethical choices. I believe that information and discussion beyond rules and regulations can help them do that. But for those who choose not to abstain, I am also concerned that they take responsibility for themselves and their partners in order to do least harm. To do this, they must have information and access to condoms and other methods of contraception. They also need access to adults who will talk to them beyond rules and regulations *and* who will not take advantage of them sexually. An adult who has clear boundaries, is willing to listen and impart solid information and discuss ethical dilemmas, and will take the time to be with young people without sexualizing the interaction is a vital resource in their sexual development.

Whatever our age, we must realize that the capacity to experience sexual intimacy with another person carries with it enormous responsibility because there are consequences for myself and the other person. The law will not allow me to drive a car without training and a license, because driving a car gives me the capacity to hurt myself and others. The law, although it establishes some limits on sexual activity, cannot adequately address the issues we are addressing here. It is rather a matter of thoughtful, careful, considered decision making based on an ethic of doing least harm that can guide us through these sometimes difficult choices.

8 The Sharing of Pleasure

Good is the flesh that the Word has become,
good is the birthing, the milk in the breast,
good is the feeding, caressing and rest
good is the body for knowing the world. . . .

Good is the body, from cradle to grave,
growing and aging, arousing, impaired,
happy in clothing, or lovingly bared,
good is the pleasure of God in our flesh. . . .

—Brian Wren, *Good Is the Flesh*

To share the power of each other's feelings is different from
using another's feelings as we would use a kleenex. When we
look the other way from our experience, erotic or otherwise,
we use rather than share the feelings of those others who participate in the experience with us.

—Audre Lorde, "Uses of the Erotic"

Guideline #4. *Am I committed to sharing sexual pleasure and intimacy in my relationship? My concern should be both for my own needs
and those of my partner.*

∞ THERE ARE A NUMBER of good reasons to interact sexually
with a partner. Sexual contact can provide comfort, pleasure,
physical release, increased intimacy, and the possibility of

procreation if we so choose. And of course, sex can be fun. But what is the connection, if any, between sexual activity and intimacy in relationship?

In an article on intimacy by clergymen Eric James and Bernard Lynch, they tell this story: "I said to a former Justice of the High Court over breakfast, 'How would you define intimacy?' He responded immediately, 'Intimacy is penetration of the vagina by the erect penis. If there is no erection, there is no penetration and if there is no penetration, there is no intimacy.' This said, we got on with our eggs and bacon."[1] This is the patriarchal, legal, heterosexual definition of intimacy: brief, narrow, and inadequate. Sexual activity of all kinds in the context of a relationship (short-term or long-term) has something to do with intimacy, that is, with opening oneself physically and emotionally to give and receive. It also has the potential for recreation and play which are very important aspects of an intimate relationship.

Feminist theologian Mary Hunt makes this observation: "Sex is not necessarily intimate, and intimacy is not necessarily expressed sexually. For some women, and for many men, the separation of sex from intimacy is welcome."[2] True, sexual activity has been equated with a romanticized notion of lifelong love and devotion which may have stifled pleasure and play. But the risk in the separation of sex from intimacy is always the trivialization of sexual activity, where, as Hunt notes, "Sex for some people is no more intimate than fast food, just another commodity which can be bought or bartered, . . ."[3] In this instance, sexual activity loses its erotic quality that grounds us in the meaning of life and life together. Peter, one of the brothers in David James Duncan's novel, *The Brothers K*, experienced this loss in a sexual encounter:

> Well, yeah, it was fun, I guess. But the trouble, see, was that we knew we didn't love each other. So even though we got excited and all, it came down to a matter of, I don't know, not mauling each other exactly, but just sort of *operating* each other. Like a couple of cars or something. Yeah, that's about right. It was like

we'd each invented this car, see. But there was no way of seeing
how well our two cars ran without her getting into me and me
getting into her and each of us test-driving each other. So that's
what we did. We test-drove our cars. And we *were* our cars.
Which was very exciting, and confusing, and made us feel all
this gratitude and shame and wonder and embarrassment
toward each other. But when it was over, we felt way too much
the way you'd feel after test-driving a regular old Ford or Chevy
or something. You know. It was like, okay, everything runs
great, yeah you're welcome, thank you too. And that was it.
Which just isn't right. The driving itself was just too wonderful
to end up feeling like that so I won't do it again. I mean, not in
that way. I want a form of wonder that doesn't turn me into a
car. I want a wonder that *lasts*.[4]

Sometimes sex is about deep and abiding love, sometimes it is
about joy and playfulness, sometimes it is about the release of
physical tension, sometimes it is about procreation—sometimes it
is about all of these things at once. It is always about relationship
to another person and to ourselves. If we lose sight of this fact, we
run the risk of exploiting or being exploited.

Song of Solomon: What Does the Bible Say About Pleasure?

The entire Song of Solomon in Hebrew Scripture is a celebration
and affirmation of joyful, pleasurable sex. The poem begins with
the woman's longing for her lover:

Let him kiss me with the kisses of his mouth!
For your love is better than wine,
　　your anointing oils are fragrant,
your name is perfume poured out;
　　therefore the maidens love you.
Draw me after you, let us make haste. (1:2–4)

In chapter 4, he then describes her:

How beautiful you are, my love, how very beautiful!
Your hair . . .
Your teeth . . .
Your lips . . .
    your mouth . . .
Your cheeks . . .
Your neck . . .
Your two breasts . . .
Until the day breathes
    and the shadows flee,
I will hasten to the mountain of myrrh
    and the hill of frankincense. (4:1–6 NRSV)

And in chapter 5, she describes him:

My beloved is all radiant and ruddy,
His head . . .
His eyes . . .
His cheeks . . .
His lips . . .
His arms . . .
His body . . .
His legs . . .
His appearance . . .
His speech . . . (5:10–16, NRSV)

The unabashed and explicit eroticism of this poem is a surprise to many who have assumed that Hebrew and Christian Scriptures are anti-sexual.

I had put off my garment;
    how could I put it on again?
I had bathed my feet;
    how could I soil them?
My beloved thrust his hand into the opening,
    and my inmost being yearned for him.

I arose to open to my beloved,
    and my hands dripped with myrrh,
my fingers with liquid myrrh,
    upon the handles of the bolt. (5:3–5 NRSV)

How fair and pleasant you are,
    O loved one, delectable maiden!
You are stately as a palm tree,
    and your breasts are like its clusters.
I say I will climb the palm tree
    and lay hold of its branches.
Oh, may your breasts be like clusters of the vine,
    and the scent of your breath like apples,
and your kisses like the best wine
    that goes down smoothly,
    gliding over lips and teeth. (7:6–9 NRSV)

Interestingly, throughout the Song of Solomon there is no mention of procreative purpose nor are the woman and man described as being married. There is no suggestion of a dominant/submissive relationship, but rather a peer relationship: "This is my beloved and this is my friend, . . ." (5:16)* The entire poem describes recreative sex with the singular purpose of sharing the passion and pleasure of a relationship between equals. It is tragic that this pleasure-affirming aspect of the Hebrew tradition has been lost or withheld from Christianity for so long.

Sexual Sharing

This discussion about sexual sharing presupposes the groundwork laid in the previous chapters. Within a peer relationship, with authentic consent, and with care to prevent disease and unwanted pregnancy, sexual sharing for the purpose of pleasure and intimacy is a vital part of an intimate relationship. Sexual

* This is surprising given that this poem was written in a cultural context that was patriarchal.

sharing is valid and can be pleasurable with or without genital contact, with or without orgasm. "Foreplay," traditionally understood as physical contact which precedes and prepares for sexual intercourse, is an unfortunate term because it belittles the pleasure and value of non-genital sexual play.

Orgasm is "the intense feeling of physical pleasure that human beings experience at the climax of sexual stimulation."[5] The experience of orgasm differs for men and women—and also for individuals—but both sexes can experience intense pleasure and physical sensation that accompany genital stimulation.

It is important to remember that in sharing pleasure with a partner, the guideline which highlights consent is very important. The particular activities that one may desire with or from one's partner may not be consistent with those of the partner. For example, if I want to have oral sex with my partner but she does not, then I must forego that particular method of sexual sharing. She may be open to exploration but then decide that she has a particular preference. I must respect her preferences. Once again, communication is essential.

Christian Scripture discusses sexual sharing and consent. For example, in discussing heterosexual marriage in I Corinthians, Paul says:

> The husband should give to his wife her conjugal rights, and likewise the wife to her husband. For the wife does not have authority over her own body, but the husband does; likewise the husband does not have authority over his own body, but the wife does. (I Corinthians 7:3–4 NRSV)

Both partners have the right to engage in sexual activity and to refuse sexual activity.* Even conservative Christian authors Tim and Beverly LaHaye agree on this issue. Quoting Dr. Herbert J. Miles in reference to heterosexual marriage, they say: "'*All sex*

---

* It is interesting that Paul makes this point of the equality of consent in sexual activity so clear in the context of the patriarchal culture in which he wrote.

experiences should be those which both husband and wife want.
Neither, at any time, should force the other to do anything that
he [sic] does not want to do. Love does not force.'"6

Paul's instruction is also a reminder that both partners have
the responsibility to attend to the sexual needs of the other: "Do
not deprive one another except perhaps by agreement for a set
time, to devote yourselves to prayer, and then come together
again, so that Satan may not tempt you because of your lack of
self-control." (I Corinthians 7:5 NRSV) Paul is advocating attention to each other's sexual needs except when the two partners
agree to a period of abstinence for a particular reason, for example, during illness or a physical separation. Paul is most concerned
about the possibility of a partner's wandering eye if her/his sexual
needs are not being met by her/his partner. I am more concerned
with the inattention to the other's needs in general. We have all
heard stories and perhaps had experiences of partners who, after
they have had an orgasm during lovemaking, roll over and go to
sleep, completely ignoring the needs of the other person. Perhaps
we have viewed this as insensitive and uncaring. Rarely have we
considered it a question of ethics.

In a just relationship, it is very appropriate for me to assert my
sexual needs and desires with my partner; and it is also my responsibility to seek to meet my partner's needs. Since in genital sexual
sharing, simultaneous orgasm is rare,7 the focus on genital stimulation needs to alternate between partners. On some occasions,
one partner may chose not to be stimulated to orgasm but rather
to experience non-genital contact and affection. The essence of
my responsibility is to remember that sexual sharing is giving *and*
receiving. I should try to be clear about what I want to receive
and try to give to my partner what she wants.

There is one important exception that should be noted here.
My responsibility to give and receive sexual intimacy with my
partner does not include doing something which I find
distasteful or offensive just because she requested it. Nor does my

responsibility include doing anything physically injurious to her just because she requested it, as may be the case in some sado-masochistic practices. In fact, my responsibilty requires the opposite. To do least harm means exactly that—regardless of the particular requests of one's partner.

Masturbation

Of course one's sexual needs and desires do not always coincide with those of one's partner. Under these circumstances, masturbation is an appropriate means of providing self-pleasure and comfort. If one is in an intimate relationship with another person, masturbation is no replacement for the intimacy which sexual sharing can provide, and should not be used to punish one's partner by withholding sexual contact out of anger.

Contrary to folklore and cultural prejudice, masturbation is natural, healthy, and commonly practiced by men and women. "Studies now report that almost all men and most women have masturbated at some point in their lives and that many masturbate throughout their lives."[8] Masturbation is an important part of childhood and adolescent sexual exploration and development and should not be discouraged. Parents should not prohibit their children from masturbating, but should help them learn that it is an activity reserved for private time and place.

Masturbation is also an important aspect of sex therapy, especially for women. "Since the main reason women seek the advice of sex therapists is orgasmic dysfunction, teaching women how to masturbate and pleasure their own bodies is usually essential before women can fully accept sexual pleasure and stimulation from others. Most sex therapists believe that it is necessary for women with orgasmic dysfunctions to learn to take responsibility for their own orgasm before they can become orgasmic from their partner's stimulations, whether manual, oral, or penile."[9]

Fortunately, some denominational policies and curricula are helping to challenge traditional taboos against masturbation. For example, The Evangelical Lutheran Church in America study materials published in 1991 said this:

> Many people have received the message that they should feel shame and guilt about touching themselves, and especially about genital self-stimulation. Today we know that such messages can be unhelpful for subsequent sexual development and relationships. . . . When practiced in private, masturbation is not unhealthy, unless it becomes compulsive or a way to avoid expressing sexual intimacy with one's partner.[10]

The most fundamental ethical question about masturbation is, does it cause harm to self or other? This is the question that the Lutheran study addresses. Like every human behavior, masturbation has the potential to be harmful. But it need not be. Masturbation can be an integral aspect of a healthy sexual relationship whether practiced alone or with a partner. It can be a useful way to share pleasure and affirm one's bodily self.

Pornography?

Is sharing pornography sharing pleasure in a relationship?* I cannot adequately discuss the issue of pornography as an ethical, social and legal question here. But I do want to speak about pornography as an ethical issue in intimate relationships. To do so, we must refer once again to our original question: how do I do least harm to myself and my partner? Does the use of pornography do harm to one's self or to one's partner?

There is no definitive answer to this question but in a culture in which male sexuality is predicated on dominance and on the

---

* By pornography, I am referring to the sexually explicit materials (print and video) available for sale, in which women and sometimes men (and children in the case of child porn) are depicted in ways which are humiliating, debasing, and often involve violence and abuse. I do not include sexuality education materials in this category.

objectification of the other person and in which female sexuality is based on submission and is generally demeaned, sexually explicit materials generally reflect and promote these values.[11] This is not good news for men or for women. Stoltenberg unequivocally describes the bad news:

> I want to speak to those of us who live in this setup as men and who recognize—in the world and in our very own selves—the power pornography can have over our lives: It can make men believe that anything sexy is good. It can make men believe that our penises are like weapons. It can make men believe— for some moments of orgasm—that we are just like the men in pornography: virile, strong, tough, maybe cruel. It can make men believe that if you take it away from us, we won't have sexual feelings.
>
> But I want to speak also to those of us who live in this setup as men and who recognize the power that pornography has over the lives of women: because it can make us believe that women by nature are whores; because it can make us believe that women's body parts belong to us—separately, part by part— instead of to a whole real other person; because it can make us believe that women want to be raped, enjoy being damaged by us, deserve to be punished; because it can make us believe that women are an alien species, completely different from us so that we can be completely different from them not as human as us so that we can be human, not as real as us so that we can be men. I want to talk to those of us who know in our guts that pornography can make us believe all of that. We know because we've watched it happen to men around us. We know because it has happened in us.[12]

Stoltenberg is describing the impact of pornography as it reflects and promotes dominant and submissive relationships between people. But he also describes the power that pornography has on individuals.

The central ethical issue in this book that relates to pornography is consent. The consumption of pornography and its use in relationships raises consent questions. There are many stories from women who have been coerced into sexual activity by partners who saw or read about a particular activity which they then required their partners to imitate. One example emerged from a review of Peter Kramer's book, *Listening to Prozac*. The review describes a patient from the book, Sam, nearly forty years old, who suffered from depression. Kramer prescribed Prozac which resulted in dramatic relief for Sam from the depression.

> But a detail of the "cure" troubled Sam. He had previously prided himself on his independent style in sexual matters. A central conflict in his marriage had been his interest in porno-graphic videos, *which he had insisted his wife watch with him* [italics mine]. But once Sam was on Prozac he lost interest in pornogra-phy (though he enjoyed sex as much as ever). The style Sam had nurtured and defended for years now seemed not a part of him but an illness. Rather than expressing independence of spirit, his sex style was a biological tic. Although Sam was grate-ful for the relief Prozac had given him from his depression, he was disconcerted because it had also redefined something that had *seemed essential about his own personality* [italics mine].[13]

Both the author and reviewer appear to accept the fact that Sam viewed forcing his partner to use pornography as his right and privilege and as essential to his being. We can assume that no one bothered to ask his wife about it, but I expect that she was delighted with the results of his therapy. Hopefully it brought her relief from sexual activity (including watching pornographic videos) to which she may have submitted but did not consent.

The production of pornographic materials also raises consent issues: do the sex workers who pose for photos or videos have gen-uine economic options? How many are literally forced to do this work? This particular aspect of the issue is controversial and hotly debated even among feminists. Any possible resolution of these questions is beyond the scope of this book, but the circumstances which relate to the production of pornography in a multi-billion dollar industry raise legitimate ethical questions for discussion.

Is it possible to imagine non-exploitative erotica in which women (and men) are not humiliated and victimized for the entertainment of others? Perhaps. But in our culture at this point in time, it is hard to imagine because most of the sexually explicit material produced in this industry still reflects and reinforces the dominant sexual themes of our society. It seems there is not a lot of money to be made in portraying equality, respect, care, and safety in sexually explicit settings.

The one thing that women and men of conscience can do about pornography is to avoid using it in their sexual relationships. Doing least harm remains the pivotal concern for me. I am waiting for proof that pornography as we know it does not do harm. If there is any chance that its use in an intimate relationship is nonconsensual, that it separates rather than increases intimacy between people, that it alienates rather than brings us more fully to ourselves, then why use it? Beyond our personal choices, the discussion of the larger social issue is complex but nonetheless requires our attention and critical thought as we look for ways together to encourage doing least harm in sexual relationships and in our communities.[14]

Sharing Pleasure Without Harm

Once again we might pause to wonder, is it possible? Is it possible to share sexual pleasure with another person without harm? Stoltenberg asserts that it is:

> Let's assume that there exists an authentic erotic potential between humans such that mutuality, reciprocity, fairness, deep communion and affection, total body integrity for both partners, and equal capacity for choice-making and decision-making are

merged with robust physical pleasure, intense sensation, and brimming-over expressiveness. Let's say that some people have actually already experienced that erotic potential and some people have never. Let's say, further that the experience of this erotic potential occurred quite against the odds—because given the prevailing social values about sex, it could not have been predicted that two people would ever find out that this erotic potential exists. . . . But as luck would have it, a few folks happen upon an erotic potential that is actually rooted in the same values that bring kindness and exuberance and intimacy to the rest of their life.[15]

These assumptions are based on the willing acceptance of the gracious gifts of sexuality and sexual intimacy which God has given us and a vigilant effort to avoid guilt, domination, objectification, and exploitation. As we seek to live our intimate lives justly, we may discover the joyful rewards of pleasure and intimacy which can result.

The possibility of sexual sharing without harm is never simple, but it is real under the best of circumstances, and even under circumstances which are less than ideal. It does of course take time, patience, and intentionality. Judith Herman observes:

Sexual intimacy presents a particular barrier for survivors of sexual trauma. The physiological processes of arousal and orgasm may be compromised by intrusive traumatic memories; sexual feelings and fantasies may be similary invaded by reminders of the trauma. Reclaiming one's own capacity for sexual pleasure is a complicated matter; working it out with a partner is more complicated still. Treatment techniques for post-traumatic sexual dysfunction are all predicated upon enhancing the survivor's control over every aspect of her sexual life. This is most readily accomplished at first in sexual activities without a partner. Including a partner requires a high degree of cooperation, commitment, and self-discipline from both parties.[16]

We are reminded that we cannot assume (take for granted) or presume (act on what we take for granted) when it comes to sexual sharing. We must continually search for ways that both we and our partner have the option to choose in sexual interaction.

If we genuinely preach and seek to practice an incarnational theology, which means that we believe that our bodily selves are a good gift from God, then we must also affirm sexual pleasure as good and, if we so choose, seek to share that pleasure in relationship. The ethical concern which this affirmation calls forth is our responsibility to attend to our own and our partner's sexual needs in a context of choice, consent, and respect.

9 Faithfulness

Love doesn't just sit there like a stone, it has to be made, like
bread; remade all the time, made new.

—Ursula K. Le Guin

Guideline #5. Am I faithful to my promises and commitments?
Whatever the nature of a commitment to one's partner and whatever
the duration of that commitment, fidelity requires honesty and the keep-
ing of promises. Change in an individual may require a change in the
commitment which hopefully can be achieved through open and honest
communication.

✂ IF WE BELIEVE that relationships are worthwhile enterprises,
and if we choose to enter into an intimate relationship, then
questions of faithfulness inevitably arise. I believe that these
questions are important regardless of the seriousness of the commitment or the length of the commitment that two people make
to each other. In other words, whether you are dating someone
or have made a lifelong commitment to them, keeping faith is
an important consideration in your relationship. How do we
keep faith with an intimate partner? How do we do least harm?
These are ethical questions which shape our actions as moral
agents in relationship. Faithfulness can be fulfilled through
truthfulness, promise-keeping, attention, and the absence of
violence.

Truthfulness

Lying is about power. Lying is the way that those who have power try to keep it and that those who don't have power try to get it. In describing the experience of African-American men and women, bell hooks observes:

> Patriarchal politics not only gave black men a bit of an edge over black women, it affirmed that males did not have to answer to females. Hence, it was socially acceptable for all men in patriarchal society (black men were no exception) to lie and deceive to maintain power over women. . . . The many southern black women who learned to keep a bit of money stashed away somewhere that 'he don't know about' were responding to the reality of domestic cruelty and violence and the need to have means to escape. However, the negative impact of these strategies was that truth-telling, honest and open communication, was less and less seen as necessary to the building of positive love relationships.[1]

Hooks goes on to describe a conversation with her sister in which her sister confesses to telling lies.

> I wanted to know why. She admitted that it started with trying to gain a financial edge in her domestic life but then she found herself just lying about little things even when it was not necessary. Analyzing this, we decided that the ability to withhold information, even if it was something very trivial, gave her a feeling of power.[2]

Adrienne Rich echoes this reality: "In the struggle for survival we tell lies. To bosses, to prison guards, the police, men who have power over us, who legally own us and our children, lovers who need us as proof of their manhood."[3]

What both writers are describing is lying in the service of survival which is a familiar experience for many people-of-color, women, gays, and lesbians. Both writers are warning us about the impact that this habit can have when we are trying to build an intimate relationship with a peer: "There is a danger run by all powerless people: that we forget we are lying, or that lying becomes a weapon we carry over into relationships with people who do not have power over us."[4] So how can we be truthful and honest with an intimate partner? It is easier said than done.

Truth-telling is fundamental to building a trusting relationship. But truth-telling is not always a simple and clear-cut act. It certainly includes not intentionally deceiving the other person. But it also means not avoiding painful issues or leaving out bits of information that are important. Rich describes the impact of lying on a relationship:

> Why do we feel slightly crazy when we realize we have been lied to in a relationship? . . .
>
> When we discover that someone we trusted can be trusted no longer, it forces us to re-examine the universe, to question the whole instinct and concept of trust. For a while, we are thrust back onto some bleak, jutting ledge, in a dark pierced by sheets of fire, swept by sheets of rain, in a world before kinship, or naming, or tenderness exist; we are brought close to formlessness.[5]

Deceit destroys intimacy. You are no less deceiving me if you are having an affair and if you merely neglect to tell me, than if I ask: "Are you having an affair?" and you say "No." What if I never asked? Neglecting to provide important information also destroys intimacy. I am no less deceiving you if I conveniently forget what I said than if I lie about what I said. Either way you feel crazy. I am deceiving you if I deny what I am feeling in order to avoid the pain of facing it. This can also make you feel crazy. To try to be truthful (which takes work and isn't always accomplished in a relationship) means that things will be complicated and sometimes painful. But, as Rich reminds us, the pain of the truth can be a relief:

When someone tells me a piece of the truth which has been withheld from me, and which I needed in order to see my life more clearly, it may bring acute pain, but it can also flood me with a cold, sea-sharp wash of relief.[6]

It is important to remember the difference between pain and harm. Pain is what happens when I hurt her feelings, am thoughtless, forget our anniversary, become seriously ill and our future together becomes uncertain, honestly say that I don't like her new haircut or the fact that she is considering a job offer in another state. Harm is when I do something that damages or breaks the bonds of our commitment such as lying to her (which is usually in an effort to avoid pain, mine and/or hers), breaking a promise, threatening her, or physically assaulting her; anything that violates trust or literally causes injury to her.

Truthfulness doesn't mean using information as a bludgeon to intentionally hurt my partner. It doesn't mean demanding information from her in order to control her actions. If I am trying to be truthful in my relationship, then I ask myself these questions: *What is it that I am avoiding telling her in order to avoid reality and the pain it may cause for me?* I might say, "No, I'm not angry," when I am, but don't want to deal with it. *What is it that she needs to know in order to deal with reality?* I may say, "I'm in a really bad mood and it has nothing to do with you so don't take it personally," or "I really need some time alone right now so I'd like to take a few days off on my own." Neither of these pieces of news is particularly welcome, but at least they help make sense of what is happening. They are painful but not harmful. Being faithful means trying, day in and day out, to be truthful with my partner. Anything less means that trust is broken, intimacy is diminished, and harm is done.

Finally, truth-telling is not only an issue between two intimate partners; it is also an issue between the couple and their community. It is very difficult for an intimate relationship to survive and thrive in secrecy and isolation. A relationship needs the context of community to provide it with support, a reality check, encouragement, affirmation, and, when necessary, challenge. Heterosexuals generally experience this supportive context on many levels (particularly when they are married to each other): family, friends, and co-workers as well as media, religious institutions, and public policy generally provide support and affirmation for heterosexual relationships. It is much more difficult for gays and lesbians. There are virtually no institutional supports for our relationships. We look to our communities and friends with whom we can be open for support.

For gays and lesbians who are closeted and who are fearful of losing jobs, housing, or custody of children, there are good reasons to keep an intimate relationship secret. Homophobic prejudice and discrimination are toxic and dangerous. But it is critical that you find someone with whom you can be open about your relationship. It may be one other couple, one friend at work; it may be a church or synagogue that is open and affirming of gays and lesbians; it may be your softball team. Find somewhere that your relationship can be acknowledged and affirmed.

If any of us enters into a relationship that we feel must be kept entirely secret, something is wrong. It means that we have no one to talk to about the relationship, nowhere we can seek advice or reflect on our choices. This kind of isolation does not nurture a healthy relationship.

Promise Keeping

To make a commitment to another person involves making promises. These promises may be made in the formal setting of a wedding or commitment celebration, or they may be more informal. They may be clearly stated between two people or they may be understood and implied. Promises are the particulars of a relationship, the things that matter, the things that two people need to hash out and come to some agreement about if they are to fulfill their responsibility of faithfulness to each other. We make promises about how we will handle money, whether we want to have children, where we will live, how we will share our household tasks, whether we will be sexually monogamous or not. The promises we make about these kinds of issues differ according to culture and individual preferences. Some couples merge their money, some keep it separate; some couples want children, others don't; some people live in the same household, others live in different cities; some couples share household tasks, others designate one partner as primary caretaker of the house; some couples reserve their sexual activity only for each other, others are comfortable having sex with someone outside their primary relationship.* Each couple needs to come to terms with issues such as these and invariably this will require compromise for both people. Once the issues are resolved, whatever promises are made need to be made with the intention of being kept.

It is never possible to anticipate everything at the beginning of a relationship. Sometimes issues arise later on which require working through, hopefully to some resolution. But also, as playwright and author Lillian Hellman once said, "People change and forget to tell each other." Two people cannot and should not promise that they will never change, that they will always be who they are today, that they will always feel the same about each other today and forever. This romantic notion is superficial at best and potentially destructive to a long-term relationship at worst. But we can promise to try to tell each other as we change

---

* For many people, a commitment to sexual monogamy is an extension of their religious values. Monogamy is a good idea these days. Not only is it the best way to insure safer sex, for many people it provides a way to focus their emotional and sexual energy in ways that are most fulfilling. It is also practical: given limited time and energy, it is simply easier to manage intimate involvement with only one other person. I agree with Rita Mae Brown who says that "Monogamy is contrary to nature but necessary for the greater social good." (*Starting from Scratch*) But this is an issue that needs to be negotiated in each individual relationship.

so that we stay genuinely present in the relationship. That is a promise worth keeping and one which will do least harm to ourselves and our partner.

Some people agree to an annual review of their relationship (around an anniversary or some other time of the year) as a way to check in and determine if there are things that need renegotiating. For example, if I have been in charge of cooking and my partner has been in charge of clean-up for the past year, I may be ready to renegotiate this arrangement because I am tired of cooking every night. Or if we have agreed to be sexually monogamous, we may choose to revisit that decision either to change it or reaffirm it. Or if I want to stop working and return to school, this will require a renegotiating of our agreement that we contribute equally to the financial maintenance of our household. Paying attention to these changes and having an agreed upon mechanism for discussion can help us keep our promises as an act of faithfulness.

Attention

Faithfulness in an intimate relationship requires attention. Relationships don't just happen nor are they sustained by one person alone. It takes two people who are paying attention. Don't confuse attention with jealousy and control. These are the signs of an abusive relationship. Attention also doesn't mean that I have to know everything. My partner's privacy is important too. Attention means that I am aware of my partner and her activities and needs, that these things matter to me, that I am available to listen, to be as supportive as possible, and that I can expect this attention from her to my needs as well. This does not mean that I dedicate my life to taking care of her. She can take care of herself and would prefer to. What I have to guard against is taking her and our relationship for granted.

It is a great temptation to let work preoccupy us, and we can easily convince ourselves that closing a big deal, redecorating the bathroom, finishing a book, working overtime to make extra money, winning a case, or saving the world are more important than our partner's needs, at least for the moment. Anything can preoccupy us in ways which distract us from our partner: our issues with our extended families, a hobby that becomes somewhat obsessive, parenting, religious activities, a political cause, or other friendships.

Having lifted up a caution about these distractions, I also want to make a plea for balance. None of these distractions are inherently bad for a relationship. In fact, they can all be important dimensions of our lives and can enhance a relationship. The important thing is keeping the balance and remembering to pay attention to our intimate relationship as well. There will certainly be times when we will be distracted by necessity. When my parent is ill and in need of caretaking, when I have a deadline to meet on an important project, during the World Series, it is appropriate to ask my partner and my relationship to make space for me to focus elsewhere for awhile. But I shouldn't make it a habit over time. When I do, if I am honest with myself, I realize that I am really avoiding my relationship. I have to make time for it, focus on it all along the way, if I am to be faithful.

The Absence of Violence

Faithfulness in an intimate relationship means no violence. Period. To use physical force, to threaten, intimidate, or frighten an intimate partner is an act of infidelity. Nothing destroys the trust in an intimate relationship quite as thoroughly as violence. If you can't trust your partner not to hit you, what can you trust?

The Psalmist knew the profound impact of violence on a relationship when he wrote:

It is not enemies who taunt me—I could bear that;
it is not adversaries who deal insolently with me—I could hide
from them.

But it is you, my equal, my companion, my familiar friend,
with whom I kept pleasant company;

we walked in the house of God with the throng.
(Psalm 55:12–14 NRSV)

To experience violence at the hands of someone you love, to be afraid of that person, is perhaps the most profound of betrayals. There is *no* excuse for violence in an intimate relationship. A commitment not to use violence in an intimate relationship is the cornerstone of faithfulness. (The obvious exception to this assertion is the use of physical force for self-defense in the face of being physically attacked by one's partner. Defense of self or of children is certainly justified. But if this becomes necessary, the intimacy and trust of the relationship have already been destroyed.)

And Adultery?

Traditionally when the question of faithfulness or fidelity in an intimate relationship was discussed, it meant one thing: adultery. Frequently, the issue at stake in the question of adultery in a heterosexual relationship has been the guarantee of paternity. The purpose of a woman's sexual fidelity to one man was to insure that any offspring of hers were his. The man's sexual fidelity was never really expected. The concern for paternity has resonated throughout religious and legal tenets for centuries. It overrode considerations of safety and well-being for women and children. It made the only promise worth keeping the promise that the woman would be sexually faithful to the man. There were no expectations that he would reciprocate this promise.

This narrow, patriarchal focus remains today. In 1968, Robert Todd Lincoln Beckwith, great-grandson of Abraham Lincoln, sued his wife for divorce alleging adultery when she became pregnant six years after his vasectomy. Beckwith asked the court to rule that he was not the father, so that the child would have no claim on the family trust. Eight years later Beckwith won the divorce, but the court ruled that the child could press a claim in the future. The adultery issue here was only a question of whether or not there would be an heir to the Lincoln family.[7]

Ethically, the focus on adultery has missed the point too many times. Too often, the church has only been concerned with who had sexual contact with whom, ignoring deceit, broken promises, and abuse in a relationship. Too many battered women have heard their broken bones and concussions excused because their batterer alleged that they were having sex with someone else. These allegations are rarely true and are most often the ranting of the batterer's extreme jealousy in his effort to control his partner. It is time that we put adultery in perspective and realized that sexual fidelity is one ethical question among many others which both partners must consider if they are to be faithful in an intimate relationship.

The real ethical questions and challenges before us as we participate in an intimate relationships are much more complex and demanding than simply who slept with whom. This is not to say that this concern is not important, because it is a question that can include many of the other ethical questions discussed here. For example, a husband and wife were having dinner together and the wife reported that she had seen her gynecologist that day. She said, "The strangest thing happened. My doctor says that I have gonorrhea." She was obviously shaken by this news. Her husband looked across the table and said, "There's nothing strange about that. I've been seeing prostitutes for thirty years." He subsequently refused to get tested for HIV infection. She divorced him on the grounds of adultery.

The husband's sexual activity with prostitutes betrayed every aspect of faithfulness to his wife. He had deceived her, broken his promises to her, not attended to her well-being, and endangered her life by engaging in unsafe sex with someone else. His refusal to get an HIV test was the straw that broke the back of this relationship. The demise of this relationship came as a surprise to the community where the husband and wife were prominent and well regarded. The husband's long-standing deceit was but one indication of a relationship in which his faithlessness was multifaceted.

My hope is simply that we can expand our notion of faithfulness to include the many opportunities we have everyday to keep faith with our partner. If we try to tell the truth, keep our promises, stay attentive, and forgo the use of violence in an intimate relationship, we will certainly enhance the quality of life between us and insure that we will do the least harm to one whom we love.

Afterword

> We have to recognize that there cannot be relationships unless there is commitment, unless there is loyalty, unless there is love, patience, persistence. Now, the degree to which these values are eroding is the degree to which there cannot be healthy relationships. And if there are no relationships then there is only the joining of people for the purpose of bodily stimulation.
>
> —Cornel West, *Breaking Bread*

✂ FOR ALL OF US who desire to be in an intimate relationship, and for whom Ken and Barbie are inadequate role models, what is required is courage. For women and men of conscience who are not willing to accept the patriarchal norms of dominance and submission, who are not willing to compromise *our* family values, who believe that justice is as important in intimate relationships as it is in the public sphere, who long for genuine intimacy where trust, safety and respect are normative, courage is necessary if we are to find ways to be authentically in relationship. We deserve better than we have been given and we can do better if we are willing to work at it.

Being in an intimate relationship with integrity is hard work for all of us. The hurdles and challenges differ for each of us depending on our circumstances, but many of the questions we confront are the same. Perhaps we can learn from each other's experiences: for example, gay and lesbian couples may have something to teach about building peer relationships and heterosexual couples may have something to teach about parenting and its impact on an intimate relationship. Regardless of our particulars, we have much to learn about doing least harm in relationship with those we love. And the choices and questions we encounter only get more complex with each passing day.

In 1983, with the publication of *Sexual Violence: The Unmentionable Sin*, I suggested that sexual ethics would be very different if we took the reality of sexual violence seriously. I am even more convinced of this assertion today. Traditional sexual ethics have too long been shaped by patriarchal values which emphasize male property rights and control of women and offer simple answers and directives for increasingly complex problems. I believe that a process of ethical discernment based on nonpatriarchal values such as justice, respect, bodily integrity, consent, reciprocity, and fidelity requires daily effort in an intimate relationship and can reward us with integrity, authentic intimacy, and the eroticization of equality.

Consequently, I have written this book. It was the hardest book I have ever written for several reasons. First, I wanted to be as clear as possible about the issues I presented and my thinking about them. This was not always easy to do. Second, I hesitated at the bad news that I had to present in this discussion about intimacy and sex in a love relationship. Perhaps the problem is this: the romantic and sentimental treatment of relationships has denied people the opportunity to deal with the bad news, the reality, with which most people are struggling. I felt a responsibility to tackle this truth-telling head on, even though I was saddened at times to be the bearer of bad news. Third, I realize that even though the title of this book is *Love Does No Harm*, I had very little to say about "love." Because the word has been so overused and misunderstood, I wanted to use other words to describe the values required for a good relationship. But Paul's brief but essential treatise on love in I Corinthians 13 remains foundational to this discussion of relationship. In spite of all of this, I persevered in order to offer the good news and the bad in a way that both challenges and empowers.

The context of violence both inside and outside of intimate relationships is the bad news we must face. Many men deny this reality and any responsibility for it. Some women engage in active denial as a way of coping with this reality. Both argue that women are not the powerless, pathetic victims they have been painted as in recent literature. This reaction to efforts to name and address violence against women is the backlash we are hearing from some women writers such as Camille Paglia and Katie Roiphe. Their strategy is to claim that men's violence against women doesn't really happen. Would that it were so easy. But denial doesn't change a pattern as deeply ingrained in this culture as men's violence against women anymore than it can stop a hurricane that is bearing down on land. Of course, not all men use physical force and coercion in their intimate relationships. Moreover, as women, we are not all victims nor are those who have been victimized always and forever victims of male violence. Women resist victimization everyday—at home, at work, at school and on the street. Of course, as women, we have power and resources, but our power is clearly circumscribed by male power which always has the option of force to gain its own way. As many women know, when we do confront or challenge men's violence, we suffer the consequences. For women or men not to face these facts of life is to risk our futures and our relationships.

There are some who will critique this book as the product of white, North American privilege, suggesting that it is a privilege to even be able to reflect on such "personal" issues when many people don't have enough food to eat or a place to sleep. I would argue that such a position assumes that those who do not have adequate material resources are not confronted with questions of sexual ethics in intimate relationships or are not capable of reflecting on them. In fact, wherever I have traveled, I have found women and men concerned and struggling with these very questions regardless of their race, class, or nationality. They may describe their particular problem or experience differently than I describe mine but they are nonetheless struggling with issues of power, of consent, of reproductive choice, of AIDS, of pleasure and its place in relationship, and of what it means to be faithful. These issues are not frivolous, but are directly tied to issues of economic development, health, the role of religious teaching and culture, legal issues, women's right to self-determination and education, and material well-being across national boundaries.[1] Again we have much to learn from each other.

Is there good news? Is there hope for intimate relationships? Yes, if we can keep our eyes open, avoid sentimentality, expect the best from each other, be patient with each other, and be willing to swim against the tide.

The way things are is not the way they have to be.
Do not accept it because your mother did.
Perhaps she did what she had to do then.

Do not follow unquestioning in your father's footsteps.
He may have chosen a path you do not want.
You must do what you can do now. You must choose for yourself.

Someday sexuality will be celebrated and shared as God's gift by all people.
Someday equality will be an erotic experience and violence will be abhorred.
Someday people will choose one another freely and rejoice in their choosing.

That day is within our reach.
We need not wait for another life, another incarnation, another generation.
In the dailiness of our lives, with those we love, we can do this differently.

Notes

Preface

1. Sarah Nelson, "Shopping for a Man," *Glamour* (March, 1992): 148.

1: Ethics for the Rest of Us

1. A number of research studies show that the vast majority of sexual abuse against boys is perpetrated by heterosexual males or females (C. Allen, 1991). Walter Bera, "Betrayal: Clergy Sexual Abuse and Male Survivors," *Breach of Trust*, John C. Gonsiorek, ed. (Thousand Oaks: Sage Publications, 1995). In a study presented by Leonore M. J. Simon *et al*, "Characteristics of Child Molesters," the authors note that over 80% of the sample of molesters studied had been married or in a heterosexual relationship. They do not conclude that the remaining offenders were gay. The issue of sexual orientation is not seen as an issue in this study. *Journal of Interpersonal Violence* 7/2 (June 1992): 211–25. "Sexual abuse perpetrators can be male or female, homosexual or heterosexual [or bisexual]. Most sexual abuse perpetrators, however, identify as heterosexual, regardless of the gender of their victims." Cathy Kidman, "Non-Consensual Sexual Experience and HIV Education—An Educator's View," *SIECUS Report* 21/4 (April/May 1993).

2. Judith Herman, *Trauma and Recovery* (New York: Basic Books, 1992), 112.

3. Nicola Gavey, "Technologies and Effects of Heterosexual Coercion," in *Heterosexuality: A Feminism and Psychology Reader*, Sue Wilkinson and Celia Kitzinger, eds. (Newbury Park, Calif: Sage Publications, 1993), 108–9.

4. John Stoltenberg, *Refusing to Be a Man* (New York: Penguin/Meridian, 1990), 29.

2: Doing Least Harm

1. *The Hippocratic Oath*, No. 1 of the *Supplements to the Bulletin of the History of Medicine*, copyright 1943. Text, translation, and interpretation by Ludwig Edelstein. Johns Hopkins University Press.

3: Power, Boundaries and Common Sense

1. See "Rape Free or Rape Prone," by Beryl Lieff Benderly in *Science* 82 (October 1982): 40–43, for further discussion of behaviors in a nonpatriarchal culture.

2. *Webster's New Collegiate Dictionary*, 9th ed., 1987, s.v. "vulnerable."

3. *Webster's New World Edition*, 1966.

4. Audre Lorde, "Interview by Susan Leigh Star," in *Against Masochism: A Radical Feminist Analysis*, Robin Ruth Linden, *et al* eds. (Palo Alto, Calif: Frog in the Well, 1992), 68.

5. This discussion of "lust" first appeared in *Sexual Violence: The Unmentionable Sin* (New York: Pilgrim Press, 1983), 57–58.

6. Augustine, *City of God* (London: Oxford University Press, 1963), 235–36.

4. The Particularities of Heterosexuality

1. Theodor H. Van de Velde, *Ideal Marriage: Its Physiology and Technique*, trans. Stella Browne (New York: Random House, 1930), 158–59.

2. George R. Bach and Peter Wyden, *The Intimate Enemy* (New York: William Morrow and Co., 1969), 261.

3. Alex Comfort, *The New Joy of Sex: The Gourmet Guide to Lovemaking for the Nineties* (New York: Pocket Books, 1991), 98–99.

4. Bernie Zilbergeld, *Male Sexuality* (Boston: Little, Brown, and Co., 1978), 49.

5. John Stoltenberg, *Refusing to be a Man* (New York: Penguin/Meridian, 1990), 34.

6. Ellyn Kaschak, *Engendered Lives* (New York: BasicBooks, 1992), 183–84.

7. June Larkin and Katherine Popaleni, "Heterosexual Courtship, Violence, and Sexual Harassment: The Private and Public Control of Young Women," in *Feminism and Psychology*, 4/2, (May 1994): 218.

8. Personal story of a former Goshen College student.

9. Larkin and Popaleni, 219.

10. Ibid. 220–21.

11. Ibid., 219.

12. Ibid., 221.

13. Ibid., 219.

14. Ibid., 222.

15. Ibid., 223.

16. Ibid. 224–25.

17. Ibid. 224.

18. Sandra Lee Bartky as cited in Nicola Gavey, "Technologies and Effects of Heterosexual Coercion," in Heterosexuality: A Feminism and Psychology Reader, Sue Wilkinson and Celia Kitzinger, eds. (Newbury Park, CA: Sage, 1993), 96.

19. Kaschak, 184–85.

20. Stoltenberg, 39.

21. Ellen Goodman, "Trying New Ways to Level the Sexual Playing Field," Seattle Times, 22 September 1993.

22. Robert Hahn, "MSV: The Newsletter of Men Stopping Violence," Atlanta, Jan., 1994.

5: Choosing Peer Relationships

1. Julia Penelope, "The Illusion of Control: Sadomasochism and the Sexual Metaphors of Childhood," in Lesbian Ethics, 2/3 (Summer 1987): 92.

2. Sheila Jeffreys, The Lesbian Heresy, (London: The Women's Press, 1994), 90.

3. Ibid., 41.

6: Authentic Consent

1. Scott Allen Johnson, Man-to-Man: When Your Partner Says No (Orwell, VT: Safer Society Press, 1992), 17.

2. June Larkin and Katherine Popaleni, "Heterosexual Courtship Violence and Sexual Harassment: The Private and Public Control of Young Women," in Feminism and Psychology, 4/2 (May, 1994): 222.

3. Nicola Gavey, "Technologies and Effects of Heterosexual Coercion," in Heterosexuality: A Feminism and Psychology Reader, Sue Wilkinson and Celia Kitzinger, eds. (Newbury Park, CA: Sage Publications, 1993), 104.

4. Ibid., 109.

5. Ibid., 111.

6. Ibid., 112–13.

7. Robert Davis, "Condom-rape Case Brings an Outcry," USA Today (October 13, 1992).

8. For discussion, see editorial "Rape and Credibility," *National Law Journal* 16/42 (June 20, 1994): A18.

9. Quoted by Sheila Jeffreys, *The Lesbian Heresy* (London: Women's Press, 1994), 40 as taken from *Sojourner* (June 1988): 5.

10. George R. Bach and Peter Wyden, *The Intimate Enemy* (New York: William Morrow and Co., 1969), 262.

11. Gavey, 102.

12. Johnson, 24.

13. "Lovesick Official Accused of Stalking," *Atlanta Journal Constitution*, 12 June 1993, p. B2.

14. Quoted in Ann Jones, *Next Time She'll Be Dead* (Boston: Beacon Press, 1994), 150.

15. For further discussion, see Wendy Maltz and Beverly Holman, *Incest and Sexuality*, (Lexington, MA: Lexington Books, 1987); and Mike Lew, *Victims No Longer* (New York: Harper & Row, 1988).

16. Ellyn Kaschak, *Engendered Lives* (New York: BasicBooks, 1992), 139.

17. Ibid, 141.

18. Johnson, 28.

19. Gavey, 103.

20. Johnson, 18.

21. Kathleen Fleming, "Checkpoint: A Lovers' Game," *Lesbian Bedtime Stories 2*, Terry Woodrow, ed. (Redway, CA: Tough Dove Books, 1990), 20–24.

22. Ibid., 24–25.

7: Stewardship of My Sexuality

1. "Man, 35, Sentenced for Infecting Lover," *Seattle Times*, 15 November 1992.

2. "Magic Johnson and the Era of Sexual Blame," Ellen Goodman, *Seattle Times*, 15 November 1992.

3. Mary E. Guinan, "HIV, Heterosexual Transmission, and Women," in *Journal of the American Medical Association*, 268/4 (22 July 1992): 520.

4. Cynthia Tucker, "Too Many Pressures on Women," *Atlanta Journal Constitution*, 16 May 1993.

5. See discussion citing Sally Jacobs in Ann Jones, *Next Time, She'll Be Dead*, (Boston: Beacon Press, 1994), 87.

6. Cathy Kidman, "Non-Consensual Sexual Experience and HIV Education— An Educator's View," SIECUS Report 21/4 (April/May 1993).

7. This story was produced in a 1994 episode of the dramatic series, "Picket Fences," on CBS-TV.

8. Sue Woodman, "How Teen Pregnancy Has Become a Political Football," *Ms.* V/4 (January/February 1995): 90.

9. The Alan Guttmacher Institute, *Sex and America's Teenagers* (New York: The Alan Guttmacher Institute, 1994), 28.

10. Woodman, 90.

11. Ibid., 91.

12. Ibid.

13. "Although the likelihood of having intercourse increases steadily with age, nearly 20 percent of adolescents do not have intercourse at all during their teenage years." The Alan Guttmacher Institue, *Sex and America's Teenagers*, 4.

8: The Sharing of Pleasure

1. Eric James and Bernard Lynch, "Intimacy: Two Articles in Apposition," *Christian Action Journal*, London, Summer, 1993), 16.

2. Mary Hunt, "On Intimacy, and Off," *Christian Action Journal* (Summer, 1993): 16.

3. Ibid.

4. David James Duncan, *The Brothers K* (New York: Bantam Books, 1992), 347.

5. Ruth Westheimer, *Dr. Ruth's Encyclopedia of Sex* (New York: Continuum, 1994), 192.

6. Tim and Beverly LaHaye, *The Act of Marriage* (Grand Rapids, Michigan: Zondervan Publishing House, 1976), 79.

7. Westheimer, 193.

8. Ibid., 174; "In *The Janus Report*, a national survey published in the United States in 1993, 55 percent of adult men and 38 percent of adult women reported that they masturbate on a 'regular' basis, ranging from daily to monthly. Furthermore, 66 percent of the men and 67 percent of the women said they agreed or strongly agreed with the statement that 'masturbation is a natural part of life and continues on in marriage.' This view was supported by 63 percent of the Catholics and 73 percent of the Jews who responded to the survey."

9. Ibid., 176.

10. *Human Sexuality and the Christian Faith*, Division for Church in Society, Evangelical Lutheran Church in America, 1991, 34–35.

11. For a current discussion of pornography and the question of harm, see Catherine Itzen, ed., *Pornography: Women, Violence, and Civil Liberties* (New York: Oxford University Press, 1992).

12. John Stoltenberg, *Refusing to Be A Man* (New York: Penguin/Meridian, 1990), 134.

13. "Curing an Illness or Transforming the Self? The Power of Prozac," a review by John Stapert, *Christian Century* 111/21 (13–20 July 1994).

14. See also *What Makes Pornography Sexy?* by John Stoltenberg, 1994.

15. Stoltenberg, 112–13.

16. Judith Herman, *Trauma and Recovery* (New York: BasicBooks, 1992), 206.

9: Faithfulness

1. bell hooks, *Sisters of the Yam* (Boston: South End Press, 1993), 22–23.

2. Ibid., 27–28.

3. Adrienne Rich, "Women and Honor: Some Notes on Lying" in *On Lies, Secrets and Silence* (New York: W.W. Norton and Co.), 189.

4. Ibid., 189.

5. Ibid., 191–92.

6. Ibid., 193.

7. Michael R. Beschloss, "Last of the Lincolns," *The New Yorker*, Feb. 28, 1994.

Afterword

1. This was certainly the case at the 1994 United Nations Conference on Population held in Cairo.

Index